BOOK VIII

DECODING SACRED FUNG SHWA

METAPHYSICAL INTERPRETATION

O.M. KELLY

COPYRIGHT

Copyright © 2023 Margret Ann Kelly/O.M. Kelly
Series: Book VIII (Revised)
First Published as Book VIII in "Decoding the Mind of God",
Margret Ann Kelly/O.M. Kelly, Copyright © 2011.

All rights reserved. This book may not be reproduced, wholly or in part, or transmitted in any form whatsoever without written permission from the author, O.M. Kelly, www.elanea.com.

The author of this book does not dispense medical advice or prescribe the use of any technique as a form of treatment for physical, emotional, or medical problems without the advice of a physician, either directly or indirectly. The intent of the author is only to offer information of a general nature to help you in your quest for emotional and spiritual well-being. In the event you use any of the information in this book for yourself, which is your constitutional right, the author assumes no responsibility for your actions.
Book ISBN: 978-0-6452492-9-3

AUTHOR

Author O. M. Kelly, known as Omni to her clients and students is an accomplished author and international lecturer, on Metaphysics, Philosophy and understanding the Collective Consciousness. Omni consults for Member States of the European Commission as a Conciliation Advisor and Rhetoric Counsellor for other International Companies throughout Europe. Omni now resides on Australia's beautiful Gold Coast, writing books, and works as a Life Mentor and Business Coach.

Omni has dedicated her life to decoding the mysteries of the universe. With a deep knowledge of the biblical agenda, mythologies including ancient Egyptology, Asian principles, and metaphysical insights, Omni has discovered the secret that all stories share a coded hidden metaphysical language. Her seminal work, "Decoding the Mind of God", is a compilation of nine volumes of metaphysical information based on the research into the coded information of the Laws of the Universe, also known as the Collective Consciousness, and represents a groundbreaking contribution to our understanding of the metaphysical universe. Now, all nine volumes are being released as separate, revised books, each offering a unique perspective on the universe's workings. Omni's work has been widely acclaimed for its depth of insight, and her contributions to the field of metaphysics have been groundbreaking.

THIS BOOK

Introducing "Decoding Sacred Fung Shwa", the revolutionary guide to understanding and harnessing the energy within your home and yourself. In this book, author O.M. Kelly (Omni), has introduced a metaphysical sixth element that takes our understanding of energy to the next level. By incorporating "Your Life Force" we gain deeper insight into the connection between our homes and our emotional well-being. Discover the power of Fung Shwa and learn how to use it to create a balanced and harmonized environment that supports your mind, body, and Soul.

The book explains the meaning of Sacred Fung Shwa to the shamanistic principles that underpin it. Delve into the metaphysical medicine wheel and explore the elements of life, before moving on to practical applications of Fung Shwa in the home.

Learn how to visualize your home as a collective energy and clear the clutter to enhance its flow. Discover your Astrological colours and how they can be used in Fung Shwa design, from the kitchen to the bedroom and beyond. Explore the compatibility of personal colours in relationships, and discover the power of paintings, pictures, and mirrors to enhance your home's energy.

But Fung Shwa isn't just about the home - we also explore its applications in the office environment and in small retail businesses. Learn how to apply Fung Shwa principles to a clothing store, shoe store, or café, even discover the role of Fung Shwa in money, and Metaphysical Numerology.

Throughout it all, we focus on the quest of life and how Fung Shwa can help you achieve your goals and live your best life. So what are you waiting for? Dive into the world of Fung Shwa and transform your home, your business, and your life today!

CONTENT

Introduction

Chapter One
The Meaning Of Sacred Fung Shwa   Page 1

Chapter Two
The Shamanistic Principles And Fung Shwa   Page 5

Chapter Three
The Metaphysical Medicine Wheel, Shamanism,
Fung Shwa And The Elements Of Life   Page 8

Chapter Four
Your House—Your Home—A Visualisation   Page 12

Chapter Five
Your Home Is Your Collective Energy—Clear
The Clutter   Page 19

Chapter Six
Your Astrological Colours   Page 21

Chapter Seven
Fung Shwa Design—Kitchen   Page 24

Chapter Eight
Fung Shwa Design—Table Shapes And Dining   Page 28

Chapter Nine
Fung Shwa Design— Lounge/Living Area   Page 30

Chapter Ten
Fung Shwa Design—Adult Bedrooms   Page 35

Chapter Eleven
Fung Shwa Design—Children's Room   Page 39

Chapter Twelve
Fung Shwa And Relationships—
The Compatibility Of The Personal Colours   Page 42

Chapter Thirteen
Paintings And Pictures　　　　　　　　　　Page 46

Chapter Fourteen
Mirrors　　　　　　　　　　　　　　　　　Page 47

Chapter Fifteen
Fung Shwa And The Bathroom　　　　　　　Page 49

Chapter Sixteen
The Laundry Room　　　　　　　　　　　　Page 51

Chapter Seventeen
The Garage　　　　　　　　　　　　　　　Page 52

Chapter Eighteen
Place The Garden Inside The House And The
House Inside The Garden　　　　　　　　　Page 54

Chapter Nineteen
Fung Shwa Your House And Garden　　　　　Page 56

Chapter Twenty
Planting Trees In The Garden　　　　　　　Page 62

Chapter Twenty One
Plants　　　　　　　　　　　　　　　　　Page 68

Chapter Twenty Two
Fung Shwa—Selling Your House　　　　　　Page 70

Chapter Twenty Three
The Old Fashioned Ways　　　　　　　　　Page 72

Chapter Twenty Four
Crystals And Cleansing A House Of Negative
Energy　　　　　　　　　　　　　　　　　Page 78

Chapter Twenty Five
Fung Shwa And The Office Environment　　Page 85

Chapter Twenty Six
Colour For The Office — Page 92

Chapter Twenty Seven
Fung Shwa—A Small Clothing Retail Store — Page 95

Chapter Twenty Eight
Fung Shwa—A Small Retail Store That Sells Shoes — Page 98

Chapter Twenty Nine
Fung Shwa—A Small Café — Page 100

Chapter Thirty
How many of you walk into a room and say "good morning" or "good night" to a room/house/office? — Page 102

Chapter Thirty One
Fung Shwa And Money — Page 105

Chapter Thirty Two
Introduction To Metaphysical Numerology — Page 124

Chapter Thirty Three
The Quest of Life — Page 127

Books by O.M. Kelly (Omni) — Page 133

INTRODUCTION

Upon the request of the "Masters of Time," I have been tasked with writing and explaining this book to you using the methods in which I have been trained. It differs from the Asian methods of Feng Shui, which involve the control of the five elements: earth, fire, wind, metal, and water by adding a sixth element "Your Life Force". I came to the realization that this interpretation is primarily designed to cater to your inner beingness. The information gently guides you towards understanding through an emotional transformation of your inner study and the behavioural patterning of the subconscious mind, located in the right hemisphere of our brain. This particular section of our brain is renowned for emitting light waves throughout, allowing us to heal our inner worlds with greater clarity. After conducting numerous seminars across the globe, many students have confided in me that they understood my explanation on a deeper level due to its subtle and gentle approach, which resonated with their emotions.

Throughout the years, I have corrected the Fung Shwa in business and homes around the world. From grand hotels in America to hospitals and medical centres throughout Europe, and even restoring old castles. I was then approached to bring the same experience to various businesses, encouraging a centred approach among the entire staff, which significantly impacted the overall productivity of the company. Additionally, I have worked on properties ranging from an old apartment in Venice overlooking the canals to a small flat in Sydney, as well as cattle stations in the Outback. Typically, my process involves walking through the front door and exiting through the back, then reversing the path and walking from the back door to the front. This mirrors the inhabitant's thinking patterns and allows me to read the internal energy of the house, leveraging the telepathic enhancement already created by the inhabitant(s).

Your home is more than just a physical space; it is a representation of your emotional intelligence and how you treat and respect yourself. As others enter your home, they read this energy unconsciously, making it important to create a harmonious space that reflects your inner self.

To add it all up: Through understanding this book of Fung Shwa, we can reprogram our mind, and bring more balance and harmony into our daily life. We are the sole – and Soul – creator of our own future. Please read on.
Omni

CHAPTER ONE

The Meaning Of Sacred Fung Shwa

Your house is your home, which is an exemplified creation of the Place or Palace where you call home and live in, as it is in service to you. Moreover, it is a representation of your emotional intelligence, revealing aspects of your inner self to others. When visitors enter your home, they unconsciously read this energy shaping their perception of how you value and honour yourself.

Chinese Feng Shui divides the world into five elements: wood, fire, earth, metal and water. With Sacred Fung Shwa, I have introduced a Metaphysical sixth element "Your Life Force". My interpretation is the next step towards the evolution of how we can understand, with more substantiation, the evolution that releases back to us through the principles of the unconscious/higher mind. The Chinese already know and have accepted what we, in the Western world, are now just beginning to learn and understand. Fung Shwa is a form of energy that comes from within. The "Fung" is the sound, and the "Shwa" is the result of that sound. For example, a clap means "attention!"; the sound that the clap makes, is the Fung returning to self, and the vibration that comes from the clap is the Shwa – the Shwa is the result of the Fung. Each time I clap my hands, that clap is a symbol of the relationship between you and me, and this vibration allows me to hold your attention. When we hold our attention, we are focused and waiting in anticipation for the next movement.

To further explain, Fung Shwa energy comes from within; it is the same as our life force. In Feng Shui, the life force is referred to as "Chi", which is the energy that flows through everything in the universe, including human beings. In some cultures, the life force of the universe is called "Chi", "Prana", or "Mana", while others refer to it as the "Force", "Universal Energy" or "Life Energy". Regardless of the name, this energy is the driving force behind all things. The universe is full of energy and life. Every single thing in the universe is made up of energy, including humans, animals, and even inanimate objects. This energy is called the life force of the universe. The life force of the universe is the energy that flows through everything, connecting all things in existence. This energy is the source of all life and creation, and it is responsible for the movement, growth, and evolution of everything. The life force of the universe is not limited by time or space. It exists everywhere and at all times, flowing through the universe reminiscent of an endless river. By learning to connect with and harness this energy, we can tap into the infinite potential of the universe and create a life full of abundance and fulfilment.

This energy is the source of all life and creation, which is responsible for the movement, growth, and evolution of everything. The life force of the universe is not limited by time or space. It exists everywhere and at all times, flowing through the universe reminiscent of an endless river through to the smallest brook. It finds its own strength through climbing over rocks, sliding down embankments, picking up its own speed and knows how and where to calm itself when its own pressure becomes entangled. By learning to connect with and through harnessing this energy, we can tap into the infinite potential of the universe and create a life full of abundance and fulfilment.

The life force of a human being is also known as "Chi" or "Qi" in traditional Chinese culture. It is the vital energy that flows through the body and keeps us alive. This energy flows through channels in the body called meridians. Chi is not just limited to physical health, but also affects a person's emotional and mental well-being. When chi flows freely, a person is in good health and balance. However, when the flow of chi is blocked, a person may experience physical, emotional, or mental imbalances, which can manifest as pain, illness, or emotional distress. In a Metaphysical interpretation, your Soul is your life force (your life's energy), your energy is your force field, and your force field is your aura, (the aura is the energy that is produced within your cells). Your Soul is the energy that collects from your unconscious/higher mind. Your Soul's journey is through the vibrational energy that releases through your heart, from your thoughts, which alerts the brain – whether that be positive or negative energy. This is your life force.

Fung Shwa is where we bring every aspect of our energetic light (life force) into the oneness, through the balancing of the mind, which you create in the moment. Being "in the light" means that you are forming a web – or net – of your own consciousness up into the Collective Consciousness, which through its positive behaviour relays all around the planet. Each time you think a thought in your truth, that thought attracts attention; somebody out there waits for the support of that thought. This is how the feldic (from the German word "Feld", which means "field") grid forms around the planet.

With every thought you think, you are permanently reaching out and bringing your future to you; so accept that you are the Fung! The energy of your Shwa is collected and stored in your unconscious/higher mind, not in your conscious (ego) or subconscious (emotional) minds. As we collect a thought to think, we create a vibration of energy that is collected up into the storehouse of the unconscious/higher mind, where the results are the Shwa!

Karma – or "Kha-Rha-Mha" – is the Shwa of the Fung; it is the result of your action. The more centred you become through this adjustment, the more you influence your house or your workplace; this places an added responsibility onto the whole planet, asking humanity to rearrange the thinking of the Collective Consciousness. As it is representing a higher form or level of communication.

The Chinese communicate with one another through a wonderful world of symbolism. Their alphabet is pictographic (closer to ancient cuneiform than to Western phonetic alphabet systems), and its symbolic structure is based on the Fibonacci sequence, which is collected mathematically through the golden mean. They have introduced us to a picture within a picture.

Whilst in China with a group of my students, a professor who was introducing us into their language asked for my country of birth. After I told him that I was from Australia, he proceeded to draw the character of Australia. Through that character, he was also explaining that I lived across the sea to the south, in a land of sunshine and vastness, a land of colour and brightness. I became quite homesick by the time he was finished regaling my homeland, which I had not seen for a number of years. That symbol did not only describe the word "Australia", it also created a picture that explained where the land was situated, where I was from, and what the country looked like – the small picture was so complete that no further explanations were necessary. This information is similar to how the Australian Aboriginals create their paintings as they place themselves up into their own royal behaviour, which is similar to how we prepare our mind as we collect ourselves for meditation. This empowerment releases them from the strength of their ego where they can easily slip into a state of grace and conformity to lift their mind above the earth, as their paintings are always looking down from a greater height, reminiscent of a drone.

Your Notes:

CHAPTER TWO

The Shamanistic Principles And Fung Shwa

The life force of the universe is a powerful and mysterious energy that is ever-present in our lives. By learning to connect with and harness this energy, we can tap into the infinite potential of the universe and create a life full of abundance and fulfilment.

Through the lens of metaphysics, a Shamanic understanding offers a unique perspective on the nature of the universal life force (Chi) and what it means for the human experience.

A Shaman is trained to accept and become the measurement of the emotional harmonics of all the species that have evolved on this planet. During the inheritance of our Totem, our energy fields are multifaceted; that energy then collects and builds up into a force field, which is of exactly the same mathematics as the electromagnetic fields of the planet. Every Shaman must learn to realize the frequencies that each animal, plant, or mineral commits to the Collective for them to have also inherited their earth.

We gain the ability to have that energy at our beck and call; it is our God-given right! I can work with different species for the different energies that I need, and then send them to other areas where I am asked to work through on behalf of the Collective Consciousness. I connect with those vibrations through my telepathic communication. I have the ability to vibrate them throughout different states of consciousness that are freely available and presented to me from the Collective Mind.

Throughout the Conduitive Laws of the Shamanistic principles, we are asked to use the electromagnetic fields of "Elephant" and "Whale" quite frequently, as their sound waves travel completely around the planet, which adds to our gravitational fields. They are excellent collectors of eternal energy. We need them to fortify our strength; we do not need to eradicate them! Elephant, through the Laws of

Totem Shamanic energy, represents "Knowledge", and Whale is "Conversation - Communication". Their sound vibrates to a very low frequency of around 2 megahertz, which allows it to travel along the crust of the whole planet. Those sounds are collected throughout the electromagnetic fields, which are construed correctly to the given point through the contact of the vibrations coinciding or arching with one another. Their sound or wisdom builds upon itself as it creates the spiral to be absorbed throughout the consciousness. It becomes never ending energy.

Whales create fields of light energy that can be seen from great distances, even from satellites travelling in the outer solar system. That vibration collects, and then it is forced through the next field of energy until it completes a full circuit. That is why both species can speak to one another through their unconscious/higher mind. They can hear each other's thoughts through the sonic sound that they produce, through the beat of their own heart. All species that vibrate to the same frequency can hear and understand this sonic sound.

Energy keeps us alive; at the same time, it can stagger the emission to our self, where we can sometimes feel too comfortable. So, it is with the Sacred Fung Shwa. We use the energy that is available in antimatter to create a balance of sound; to return to us through matter.

We are all responsible for this Fung Shwa, through conjoining with the program of the Collective in order to be part of the creation of the planet. This comes about through learning to understand ourselves first, which gives us the courage to release our understanding out to others. Tell this story to all your friends, and that will then allow the Shwa to go from one area to the next. Explain it in your own vibration – your own thoughts – and after you pass it to someone else, they will then pass it on through their own vibration, and so on. It is when a person refuses to acknowledge that part of the story within themselves, that the story becomes disturbed and mistranslated.

When you open that doorway of communication, you place your energy out into the Collective; this is where it is measured through the electromagnetic fields so that it can vibrate through to the mathematical Collective Inheritance of the oneness – and this is how we create and release our Truth.

Your Notes:

CHAPTER THREE

The Metaphysical Medicine Wheel, Shamanism, Fung Shwa And The Elements Of Life

Allow me to explain another version of the secrets of the Medicine Wheel. Shamanism is the supreme biological training of the mind; the myths of history are also explained to us this way. The stories are the worlds of Metaphysics – or the matter of physics – that is, our consciousness evolved through the mathematics collecting the energy of the unconscious/higher mind, which urged us to move forward through the Medicine Wheel of our body.

North = Above
The direction of north is up and forward, no matter which way we are facing. When we relate it to the body, the north begins around the neck area and goes up to the crown of the head. We enter into the north in order to grow and receive; this is the land of the invisible myth. The north is the top of the mountain; it is how the stories of the Bible were created in the first time.

The Bible is written in code for you to understand the inner you; not the planet as a whole. Do you remember the old saying, "Go north, and you will find it!"? One of my late father's sayings to me was, "Go north, and your search will find you; you can learn to release the thoughts that you have earned from understanding yourself."

South = Below
The direction of south begins through the world of understanding ourselves. In our body, the south begins with the feet and legs, and goes up to just above the navel area. South is where we have stepped into the underworld, through the worlds of our fear; it is where we go into our darkness to discover our inner light. That world was created for us through the trepidations of our forefathers and foremothers, who neither understood nor accomplished their Divine

Inheritance.

In my case, the south was where I had to learn, to earn my trust in self. It is the primordial evolution; in other words, it is the place we climb into where we overprotect our thinking. Some call this experience, "voodoo". I remember my teacher explaining to me that Sigmund Freud was a great teacher of voodoo. Voodoo is where the mind overpowers the emotions. Carl Jung was a teacher of the occult, and that is where the emotions over power the mind.

It depends on whether the left or right brain is in control in that moment. They were both right, and if we could harmonize and bring both together, we would have earned the understanding of the Oracle of Life.

East = Within
The direction of east is the story of the connection to the inner self. The east is the area of the body that begins around the heart area, going out to the release of the action of the right arm and up to the base of the throat. The Bible explains the story of the Wise Men from the East, who brought their gifts of the essences for the baby Jesus to anoint him as he lay in the manger.

The wisdom of the Collective comes from the east, which is brought through to the right hemisphere of the brain and also through the action that comes from the right hand. It is an ensuing consequence resulting in a positive intelligence. We realign with the knowledge of the Soul's intelligence. The Arabic nations use the right hand to eat their sustenance, as they are returning their blessing to themselves.

West = Without
The direction of west is the arid or empty spaces in the mind. It is the left brain and the action that comes from our left hand. In Shamanism, we go west – or into the wilderness as Eli did – to dichotomize our thoughts in order to bring all of our knowing together. Do you remember the story of Eli who went into the wilderness to attain his own inner word? This is the world of listening to the self; and, from listening, we begin to hear that which is important for us to nourish and

accept, in order to see how far we have come.

West is the last direction that we go to before we ascend into the mastering of the east, which is awoken through our own vibration confirming itself.

We gather information, and, as it filters through, it becomes our worlds within worlds, and it builds us up emotionally. I liken this to equating all the information into balancing both brains, where we have the possibilities of using our information through the harmony of both brains listening to each other as they join forces with one another where they are together forever. The light we bring forth expands through every cell that is embedded within. We can explain that story from the inner or outer – or from the logic or creative. We are all different; we use our personalities in the ways that suit our own moment.

I am mastering me, and I am always searching for more in the Collective. In other words, I am bringing energy into me; I dichotomize and release it back out again, where I become my educated mind through using my inner heavenly energy.

It does not matter which direction we face on the planet; it is the movement of consciousness in our own force fields that is the Fung Shwa. We are our own compasses, so we can create the four directions – or that Medicine Wheel within our body.

The "Western Wall", which was built on Mount Moriah in Jerusalem, is the only section of the Holy Temple that still stands after the Romans' destruction of it. That wall symbolically supports those who gather there to strengthen their own beliefs. We in the West need that support; we need it in order to believe in that which we are accomplishing within ourselves.

On a trip through North Africa to Mali, an Elder of the Touaarik tribe (this tribe is also called "Tuareg") gave me a compass that they have used for thousands of years in the desert, in order to travel from oasis to oasis. It is created in the sign of the cross. He explained how the compass works in the sand. The sand reads the shape of the compass, and the priests read the energy waves that the sand creates. The reading is construed through the mathematical vibration of the silica that is produced through the sand, where it releases the light; they explained to me that they were never lost in the desert, as the light always points them into the direction of the north.

Those High Priests have been looking after the "tomb of the books of truth" – or the ancient Library of Tumbouktu (pronounced in English as, "Timbuktu") for nearly 2,000 years; they still wear the same style of garment and symbols, and they still rely on the compass to direct them as they collect and scribe the ancient languages of the past.

Your Notes:

CHAPTER FOUR

Your House—Your Home—A Visualisation

When I began my education in order to understand Fung Shwa, I was asked to create a peaceful corner in my home. I had to spread that peace completely throughout the area I had chosen; once the peace filled that room, I had to move the peace throughout the whole house. I wanted my home to become a meditative environment; to bring me the quietness that I was yearning for. To accomplish this solitude, I was taught to begin by looking down on the room from the ceiling. It's amazing how many layers of energy you see from up there! All this energy has collected over time, building up in each room, and just by looking down from above you can see it all. So, follow me as I take you through a guided meditative tour of how I discovered my inner worlds in order to become responsible for my inner reality.

I will begin with how my Aboriginal teacher Peter explained their knowledge to me. Have you noticed how they paint their pictures, which also explains to us their inner story? It is all created with small branches of wood that they choose to paint their dots onto the bark, now it is done on cloth or canvas. They close their eyes and slip into the dreaming (similar to how we prepare our mind for meditation) through the stillness of their mind, their inner self begins to create a picture which all shaman use, no matter what country we live in, or language we speak. These pictures begin to herald a story in concordance to the women's thoughts. The deeper they go into their mind, they begin to levitate up into their next level of consciousness - the upper mind, as they feel themself rise above their body and travel towards their upper and outer boundaries, which is all relayed to them through their higher self. The picture begins to create itself, the higher they travel upwards as they could see how the layers of the land collected to build their picture that they wanted to create. These layers can take in a large area of land to assist them as they explain their story on the canvas, or for smaller objects like the animal kingdom where they found that they have the ability to read the whole animal, even down to their bone matter, in its perfect form of evolution, through their own image inside their nation, their imagination. I could see the familiarities to the cuneiform explaining their language when taking my students to China. This was how it was done thousands of years ago, as I was told. I would watch the Aboriginal women paint for hours as they told me the story of how their dreaming created their story back through to them. Their serenity was extremely calming as they dabbed their dots on to the canvas. It was an earlier form of the Metaphysical explanation that is still heralded down to this day, nothing has changed, and it all depends on the centred mind of the artist themself.

Now allow me to take you back to the beginning by asking you to walk into your lounge room, as this is the room where we like to unwind and relax. Please place yourself in a comfortable position, close your eyes, and take three nice, deep breaths – learn to expel all your jumbled thinking. It took no time for me to write that sentence; yet, accomplishing this first step may take you hours, days, or weeks – perhaps even longer for you to accomplish it with confidence and ease. More importantly, all this can only be accomplished through you trusting yourself! We begin with three breaths, although, if you notice that you have had an active day, you may need to take six or nine deep breaths to relax your mind and body.

You know you are capable of doing this, as, unconsciously, you are repeating this action thousands of times a day. We refer to this act as a "blink of the eye"! I would like you to learn to strengthen and lengthen this blink – that is all. And what do you want to do when you close your eyes upon retiring to bed? You want to rest! Important things that your ego has been confronting all day, but that have not been equated, always bring themselves to your immediate attention, as to how we allow the mind to take control and race ahead, which leaves us stranded in thought, and we feel that nothing has been finalized.

We think millions of thoughts throughout our day, and our mind begins to clutter and block up just like the drain in the kitchen sink when too much junk has been pushed down the plug hole – that is, when we are not paying attention to what we are doing.

Allow your mind to earn its freedom to release you up into another realm of thought; this is also a part of your existence that has been passed on to you through your genetic inheritance. I want to explain to you how you are able to reinvest in yourself. There are many things about ourselves that we like to keep inside, hidden from our outer feelings, and so we hang onto them for repose, but we don't want to understand them due to a lack of energy.

Well, I would like you to know that I am standing right beside you to show you the way and to inform you that you are not alone as you learn to discover this inner part of yourself. Let's start at the beginning, where we refer to this experience of "imagination", and I would like you to begin to imagine that you are lifting yourself up and ascending up to the ceiling of your room. You are quite capable of changing the old patterns of your mind; this is an added way for you to reinvest in yourself by learning something that could lift you out of your old ways of thinking. It will create a new experience for you to add to your inner dictionary of words, ideas, and results.

Relax as you allow this – have no fear, as it is quite comfortable, and there is no danger of you falling. You are learning to step onto the path that we have labelled "non-attachment"; all of which strengthens your attitude and futuristically becomes a state of tranquillity. It is a place of abeyance, a resting place, where time learns to stand still for a while, allowing you to adjust your feelings in regard to yourself. Another name for this is the first layer of unconditional "love"!

Stay up here with me, and, when you begin to feel comfortable with this experience, you can envision yourself walking very slowly through your front door and sliding up to the ceiling of the lounge room. Feel your head lightly touch the ceiling. See! There is no damage to you or your mind! Take a look around the room, knowing that you are safe to study your home from this point of view, which will enhance what you have already acclaimed for your home.

We will begin our tour of virtual reality from the lounge room.

How important does this room feel? Begin to take notice of where each piece of furniture is situated. First, look towards the door: Where are the windows situated? Can you see how much light comes into the room? What is the first thing that hits you when you walk through the door? Can you see the opposite wall? Is it clear enough for you to notice it? Is there furniture placed along this wall? Where is the lounge situated – does it look inviting as you walk into the room? You see, you can create this experience with me, as I am mentally guiding you through each phase.

As you move through each room, please learn to look at the depth, width, and volume of each piece of furniture. Take a mental note of where each piece of furniture is situated. Remember that you are up high in the room; it is as though you are walking on fluffy white clouds, and just know that these clouds will support you, with your head just slightly touching the ceiling.

Now comes an intricate part of this quest: I would like to see if you can measure your mind against the mass volume of furniture in each room. Do you feel that it is all too overpowering; is it too big and taking up too much room? Is it the opposite; is it too small? Does each piece of furniture fit the room sufficiently? Do you feel comfortable in the presence of this room, when you walk over it? Did you receive this furniture as a gift from the past? Is it an inheritance? Did someone pass this furniture on to you? Did you purchase this furniture to suit you at an earlier stage in your life? And, finally, how pleased do you feel with the results of looking into your room from above?

Now comes the next phase of this journey. I want you to notice where your energy is in that room. Are you comfortable with what you see in each room? Do you sense that it all belongs to you and your family? Can you stretch your arms out and admit that this room is yours – or do you feel that you are jammed up in a corner? We are learning to look at the mass volume that you have created, where you are able to see the energy of what you have allowed to become your home or is it a house. The most important question is simply this: Is your house your home?

It doesn't matter whether it is the depth or width of the furniture; the volume of energy that each piece of furniture consumes inside the room, is what hinders your mind. Are you satisfied with the colours that are in your room; are they compatible with one another? Years ago, when I first was introduced and educated into this information, I could not afford to change all my furniture, so I went out and bought many yards of unbleached calico, and I made slipcovers; thus, all the soft furnishings were of the same mind, and what a difference it made to the room. The rooms grew in size, and the harmony that this produced made me want to enter the rooms. I just needed an accompanying colour for the cushions and a rug on the floor to bring the room into balance. I found that if the room was balanced, so was I!

If you feel that a piece of furniture doesn't quite fit, mentally move it out and try to imagine something from another room in its place; mentally check to see if this is appropriate. You see, up here in the clouds we can do all of this! Now is the time to see how much peace and openness you can create in each room.

Can you see any discomfort of energy in any of the rooms? If the energy of the room is blocked, it will clutter your mind; a blocked thought lodges itself into a fixed position, and it stays there. You will tend to sidestep around that area. Please note that blocked energy interrupts the flow of the life force in a room, where you will create a tendency to shy away from entering into it!

Please bring your mind back into the lounge room, where we began; I want you to take another symbolic walk with me through the mind of your home. It is no longer a house. A house is something we look at; a home is something we look into, and that is so much more important! What a difference this makes to your mind! So up we go again to walk in the clouds, where we can begin to place the illusion – or a veil – over each piece of furniture. Take your time to walk through each room throughout your home again. This time, the covered furniture is no longer a sentimental reminder of someone or something; it is a veil of mass energy that consumes your time and space. The energy that is consumed by the furniture is also playing havoc with your energy, so think about how much your home is consuming you! Now don't go berserk and overcrowd the room with furniture; please allow the room its own space to breathe!

It is much easier to move from place to place if the furniture is veiled. When you veil each piece of the furniture, you can see the volume of energy that each piece consumes in each room. Now you have the choice to see if any of that furniture is worth keeping; or whether you feel free enough in your mind to release it out to the Universe. There is someone out there who could benefit through what is no longer appropriate in your life! We are now beginning to understand the methods of consuming evidence that you have allowed to emotionally attach itself to you. Is all of it worthy of you? When you are satisfied that you can symbolically see the changes that need to be made, you can remove these veils. Now we are beginning to see your home believing in itself! You are accepting how this royal aplomb will enhance not only your home but your mind as well.

Be aware of what energy is overpowering you in your bedroom. Keep this room light and free; it does not need to be cluttered and crowded with furniture. This is the area where you rest and sleep; it is where you have the opportunity to allow your light bodies, which are your Soul's veils – or, another term is "your personalities (aspects of self) that are in abeyance to you" – their time to stretch and travel around.

Now let us move on to your children's bedroom. Let us start with the younger ones. Do not choke the children's room with clutter and toys. Your child can only play with so many toys at one time. Put the rest away and periodically exchange the choice of toys, which gives them the time to reinvest in themselves. You will learn to understand which toys become a favourite with your child. And for God's sake, not too many colours – this keeps the child's mind activated where they are permanently on the go, all the time. Are you beginning to understand this dreaded discord (or dis-ease) that we have named "ADD"? These colours are reflecting through the child's sleep as well; these colours may be appealing to you, but too many colours will over activate the child's behavioural patterns. Your child is looking for a respite in their own domain. This room is supposed to represent their inner sanctuary! Soft light pastel tones rest their little minds. Strong colours become abrasive, and no lemon or yellow as this colour over activates their mind and pushes them out of their safety harness, where they become obtrusive to their inner self.

Your Notes:

CHAPTER FIVE

Your Home Is Your Collective Energy—Clear The Clutter

This chapter delves into the concept of energy and how our energy is affected by our environment, including the objects we surround ourselves with, the colours we choose, and the layout of our homes. By creating a harmonious and balanced environment, we can enhance the energy in our homes and therefore improve our lives.

How much of your time and freedom do you think your home depletes from you? Is your time consumed with cleaning? Are you searching for your own personal work area amongst the clutter of your remembrance? Where is your free domain in your own home? Have you found it yet? Your home is your own collective energy, so make it work for you – instead of you always working for it! If your home is cluttered with the past, so, too, is your mind. Stop refraining yourself! Remember while you hang onto the support of yesterday, tomorrow falters. When teaching this seminar, it was so interesting to watch the students turn their gaze up to the ceiling. I stopped talking and asked them to put down their pens and paper, close their eyes, and review their own personal situation. I left them with their visions, and was surprised at the length of time it took them to come back to the moment; when they finally did, they quietly picked up their pens and paper, and continued to write. Not one word was spoken for half an hour! Over the next few weeks, I watched as the students shared what things bothered them in their personal life.

Learn to keep your home organized; it is the little things as well as the large things that will consume a vast amount of energy in a room. It all depends on the colour and shape of the design. Bright patterns slice a room up into segments, as this disturbs the mind, which is always searching for its own solace. Accessories play an important part in any room. Put away the small, conspicuous tiddly bits, or group them into an inconspicuous place. Try to create a performing story around them, if they are that important to you.

As the child becomes nearer to adulthood, they want everything to be on standby, close at hand. They are staking their claim that this room is theirs, so do not interfere and keep out!

Now we turn our attention to paintings on the wall. Place a statue or large piece of pottery/vase near a painting. Make sure that the colours complement one another. Again, if you're interested you can pull a pronounced colour out of the painting. The walls could be painted in a pastel form announcing this colour. Can you begin to envisage how the room is collecting and forming its own energy? Fung Shwa is making you aware of how the energy rolls around a room in slow elongated waves. Do not use sharp objects in a room which is meant for relaxation. Keep each room down to two or three colours. Don't clutter! I would like to see you re-create your awareness so that it becomes an auric convocation of oneness.

Allow your unconscious/higher mind to have free rein! Notice the feeling of a sense of "loyalty which manifests royalty" overtaking your old ways, where you are becoming an added attraction to yourself. Isn't it a good feeling to feel free within your heart? Your new home will manifest for you, as it becomes your new "temple of light".

As you step from one room into the next one, make sure that the colours complement one another. It is the same as walking into the forest where subtly the trees are replaced with a new species where the view is extended as you notice the adjustment in your view.

Your Notes:

CHAPTER SIX

Your Astrological Colours

You were born at a certain time, on a certain day, in a certain month, in a certain year. That is your Astrology. You are given one of the twelve signs through your date of birth, which becomes the building blocks of your foundation; your sign is a guide to assist you in strengthening these building blocks that you have inherited, from your past generations. You have inherited their positive outlook as well as a reflection of what they could not adhere too, where the responsibility is for you to continue to support what they were too afraid to venture into. As you motivate yourself to move forward into your own direction, this creates a counterbalance which corrects their overflow where you are lifting them out of their reverie of their past which allows you to have a more favourable outcome during your inheritance. Therefore you have cleared or eradicated their past which gives you the opportunity to inherit your own true worth.

The Astrological wheel is another tool of reference that connects us into our inner mythical journey. Mythology or (metaphysically, my-theology is explaining to us as my way of life) began to explain itself back through the twelve houses of the Gods or the Twelve Houses of the Astrological Signs. It is a mirror guiding us up towards the entrance into the unconscious/higher mind. This is where we enter up into the home of the High Priest, the Sage, the Shaman, and the Prophet. They represent personalities (aspects of self) that have collected and have earned their written stories, as a result of having entered up into these higher territories (higher emotional intelligence). Now can you understand the stories from the Egyptian hieroglyphs that are carved on the walls of the temples, regarding Astrology, known as the language coming from the stars?

Your journey is an added value to your intelligence, which has manifested into its own discernment through you following the mathematics of your personal intellectuality in how you have understood or are in the process of understanding your own

Universal Law. Astrology is an introduction into the language of Metaphysics, (the matter of your physics) and it is also an explanation of how we can form a deeper relationship with our Soul's experience – that is, it is a way for us to release a sense of freedom within our self in order to add to, and work with, the experiences that automatically occur in our life. We begin by understanding the twelve signs of Astrology and the colours that we emit through our auric fields as we learn to understand the journey through them.

Aries – "I am."
Light red; light pink; white; pale grey.

Taurus – "I have."
Medium brown; beige; sand; light young green; plum; rose.

Gemini – "I think."
Grey; light blue; white.

Cancer – "I feel."
Peacock colours; rich sea-blue; blue-green; grey-green; silver; white.

Leo – "I will."
Bright sunflower-yellow; orange; gloss red; black; gold.

Virgo – "I analyse."
Chocolate-brown; rich dark green; emerald-green; green; gold.

Libra – "I balance."
Sky-blue; light blue-grey.

Scorpio – "I desire."
Green; dark blue-green; deep blue; dark red; deep purple; gold.

Sagittarius – "I see."
Noble reds; pink; royal blue.

Capricorn – "I use."
All greys; greyish, chalky browns; black; violet.

Aquarius – "I know."
Aquamarine; light blue; electric blue; blue-grey; black.

Pisces – "I believe."
Ice-blue; ice-green; deep blue; black.

Complementary Colours

Silver and gold can be used as complementary colours when you combine them with other colours. Silver represents the inner systems; through combining it, you have the opportunity to reach out into another world. It also represents the transformations of the freedom of self-discovery. Grey and light blue are mutable with silver, which means that they are secondary colours. Watch how quickly your thinking changes when you walk into a room that has silver accessories. I also relate silver to the psyche of the inner realms – it represents the soft glow of the moon, which has a calming effect to relax the "physics of the mind".

Gold is a different equation; it brings us back into the centre of the self, and it also empowers the psyche of the outer self. Gold condenses energy, and so its energy must be applied in a forthright manner. It is the focus of all, and I like to call it the "geometry of the mind". Silver is a question searching for an answer. On the other hand, gold is an answer searching for a question. Be careful with the use of gold in a room; keep it limited, as it has a direct energy and makes you live up to the thought in your moment. For compatibility to the mind, we use less gold than silver. Viewing the colour gold dehydrates the body, and it also tires you out very quickly. In the presence of the colour gold, your ego has difficulties keeping up with its own demands!

Your Notes:

CHAPTER SEVEN

Fung Shwa Design—Kitchen

Over the years, I have corrected the Fung Shwa in many homes around the globe – from an old apartment in Venice overlooking the canals to a small flat in Sydney. I usually start by walking through the front door and out the back; and then I reverse, turning around and walking from the back door to the front. This mirrors back to me the perspective of the inhabitant's thinking patterns. I learn to read the internal energy of that house, through the telepathic enhancement that the inhabitant(s) have already created. If there is no back door, like in an apartment or flat, I walk the full length of the apartment/flat, turn around, and face the front door. In this sense, I can create a mirror image of the space in my unconscious/higher mind; remember that, when we see things in reverse, we find we are looking through, not at. This is what happens with the mirror image of the apartment/flat when you do this as well. Try to see how you can convert the energy of your past by rearranging it into becoming your future home.

In reference to living in an apartment building and whether your "front door" is the door to enter the building or into your apartment the answer is: the entrance concerned is the one that you use to walk into your own apartment, as that is where your energy belongs. The energy that collects at the front door of the apartment building is a shared experience.

Energy and Fung Shwa—Kitchen

Remember that the Soul is the centre of all. If done correctly, Fung Shwa is arranged in a circle, where the energy is permanently representing harmony, balance, and freedom. If you read the room in a clockwise direction, the energy opens up the right hemisphere, where you are free to reinvest in yourself (increase your emotional intelligence). If you read the room in an anticlockwise direction, the energy opens up the left hemisphere of the brain, where you are still in a refrainment of creating further excuses for self or others.

In the rooms where I spend my time during the day (i.e., kitchen), I create a triangle inside the circle that holds the fridge, oven, and stove. That triangle begins to work for me, cutting my time down by half. Another triangle is created between the pantry, the pots and pans, and the sink area. Now we have two separate triangles which work in harmony with one another. Again, my preparation time is cut by half. In busy rooms, I like to be in, out, and over with. I am a very creative cook, so my kitchen is arranged to act in a clockwise position which will keep me tuned in to the preparation of my meals; I want to be able to rotate around the kitchen, not dart and weave from side to side, or move backwards and forwards. The energy becomes static, and then so does the mind. I want each creation to be presented to my family or guests in a stress-free situation.

We step "up" into a kitchen, so the floor should be of a lighter colour than the walls. That will make all the difference to the energy of preparing a meal. Lots of stainless steel in the kitchen enhances the mind into a form of cleanliness, where, as we use the pots and pans, we want to clean them immediately. The reflection of the pots enhances the cooking, increasing the desire to make it be more modified, more exemplified; this, of course, creates the illusion that the meal is more palatable, and so we appreciate it more when we eat it.

The meal you place on the table is perceived as atonement to the self; in other words, it is a blessing that one returns to self. If you know and feel that your kitchen is irregular, and you cannot change it, the inner mind has to become more focused; the way that we correct this behaviour is to make sure that all the ingredients needed for each dish are prepared on the bench in a clockwise motion, one step after the other. You will find that this compatibility equates and complements the meal. If each meal is complemented from the beginning of preparation, the receiver also receives the same benefit. Take notice of how the Asian continents prepare their meals; they seem to be able to multiply time, and I learned very quickly how they can prepare a succulent meal in minutes. Through my upbringing, I was trained that the evening meal was prepared straight after the breakfast dishes were put away. The day seemed to become a breeze, with no entanglements at the end of the day.

A few more guidelines for the kitchen:

- Clear the clutter: Start by decluttering the kitchen and removing any unnecessary items that may be causing stagnant energy. A clean and clutter-free kitchen creates a more peaceful and inviting space. As stated previously, stainless steel in the kitchen enhances the mind into a form of cleanliness.

- Create good lighting: A well-lit kitchen with natural light and or bright artificial lighting is important for creating good energy flow.

- Use your Astrological colours wisely for the kitchen.

- Keep the kitchen organized: Keep the kitchen organized and easy to navigate to promote good energy flow. Keep commonly used items within easy reach and avoid cluttering countertops. Use drawer and cabinet organizers to keep everything in its place.

In Fung Shwa, the pantry is considered an important area in the house as it is related to the nourishment and health of the family. Here are some guidelines on how to set out a pantry:

- Clean and declutter: Start by decluttering the pantry and getting rid of expired items. A clean and organized pantry promotes good energy flow.

- Organize by category: Organize the items in the pantry by category and store them in clear containers with labels. This makes it easy to find what you need and also creates a sense of order and harmony.

- Keep it well-stocked: A well-stocked pantry represents abundance and prosperity. Keep it well-stocked with healthy, nourishing foods to promote good health and well-being.

Fung Shwa can also be applied to the inside of a refrigerator to improve the flow of energy.

- Keep the refrigerator clean and organized. A cluttered and messy refrigerator can create stagnant energy and make it harder to find what you need. Remove any expired or spoiled food, wipe down spills, and organize items by category and use.
- Position the food strategically. Place fresh produce, dairy, and meats in the appropriate drawers or shelves. Avoid storing items in the door, as this area tends to fluctuate in temperature and can lead to spoilage. Keep the most frequently used items within easy reach and visible.
- Utilizing round containers to store cooked food as this impedes bacteria from collecting, however, consume the cooked food within the recommended time by health authorities, or expiry date.

Your Notes:

CHAPTER EIGHT

Fung Shwa Design—Table Shapes and Dining

Allow me to turn to the atonement – or "at-one-ment" – one gives oneself regarding eating meals at the table. This is a time to thank each personality (aspect of self) for the service it has rendered to the inner self! By now you are aware of my explanations regarding you being the most important person in your life!

To begin with, we used an oblong table to support the family, mother and father sat at each end, and the children sat alongside them. As the children began to grow, we had a tendency to look for an oval or round table, as these shapes makes each person at the table feel a sense of equality and the freedom to communicate with one another. This shape is a sign of respect. If you begin with a rectangle, you finish with a rectangle. If you start with a circle, you have to finish with a circle. If you start with an oval, then you finish with an oval. Everything should be geometrically harmonized and balanced. Place mats can be bought in all sizes today – rectangle, square, round, or oval – and, once they are purchased, they are on hand for use over and over again. Remember, eating releases a blessing that one gives to the self!

Find a low bowl that is the same shape as the table, fill the centre of this bowl with flowers, and then place the bowl in the middle of the table; this will define and equalize the energy. We display the flowers in the same shape as the bowl in order to gather the energy up to a point in the middle of the arrangement, which creates an antenna. What does this accomplish? It diffuses the Collective Energy, broadcasting it out into the room, in order to make the area appear lighter and larger. We use the shape of the table to enhance and create an equalized structure, which brings a sense of harmony and compatibility into the room.

In Europe, I had a large, oval dining table that was four meters long and could seat fourteen people comfortably, with plenty of elbow room. The amount of people seated determined how I decorated the table. For formal occasions, I used a tablecloth that reached the floor and was similar in colour to the dinner setting. I used three smaller oval bowls for the flowers, balancing the symmetry of the table with two large candelabra (around forty centimetres high). The candlelight flickered down from above, causing no interference as to viewing or communicating with one another across the table. When I had fewer guests (eight to ten people), I used one long oval flower arrangement in the centre, with two smaller candelabra on either side to suit the smaller group. This allowed the energy to flow and surround the table, without cutting anyone out of the conversation; in fact, it became much easier for the communication to flow.

Depending on how many people I had seated, I determined how much energy I needed to create each wave. I enjoyed seeing the energy roll around a conversation. For a group of six people, I could afford to have one large candelabrum in the centre and individual flowers in front of each place setting. This made each dinner guest feel important! I did not like to clutter the table with too much décor.

When I invited a small group of people, we conversed and ate in the winter garden, or on the patio, and I used a small round table, which enhanced the ease of conversing in compatibility with one another. No candles were necessary during the day; through respect, I gave each guest his/her own individual place setting with a tiny arrangement of flowers or buds (preferably, during the evening).

Your Notes:

CHAPTER NINE

Fung Shwa Design—Lounge/Living Area

We step "into" the lounge room – not "up" or "down". Your home is your pure energy; it is your light, wisdom, and knowledge, so we should extend the same tone throughout the house. We do not want this temple of yours to be so busy with colour that your mind is jumping from one subject to another, not knowing what to do or in which direction to flow. Try to create compatible colours throughout the house in order to create an energy flow through each doorway. Let the same colour flow through into every room. Do not ostracize one room against the other. It's your home; please allow it to form a sense of compatibility with your mind!

For my lounge room, I want a peaceful palace to relax in, where I prefer everything to rotate in a clockwise direction. This keeps the energy circulating in a wave. I want the energy to continuously roll around the room, where conversation is free to attain a state of progressive behaviour. The mind can find a languid expression which helps the body replenish from the day's activities. Once the connection has been accomplished throughout the mind, the leading progressive apostolate then has the opportunity to create the scene, where the other personalities (aspects of self) slide into a repose position without adding any further stress. Squares and rectangles, which denote a rigid mind, offer no support for the mind of someone entering the room to relax. These symbols and shapes are designed to elongate the walls, through the rectangle, with a painting or tapestry. Through a square, a wall will appear smaller.

A few more guidelines for the lounge/living area:

- Use Lighting: Lighting is also important in Fung Shwa, as it can help to create a positive atmosphere. Natural light is best, but if this is not possible, using soft lighting or lamps with warm light bulbs can help to create a relaxing and welcoming atmosphere.

- Incorporate Nature: Bringing elements of nature into the space, such as plants, flowers, or natural materials like wood or stone, can help to promote positive energy. Plants, in particular, promote positive energy and can help to purify the air. An excellent plant for the lounge area is the Aralia plant. Aralias have leaves of seven finger points; these are flat, wide, broad leaves that would allow the mind to relax just for a brief moment. These plants look like open hands with the fingers outstretched. I refer to the Aralia as my "pause plant". Lucky Bamboo: Lucky Bamboo is a popular plant that brings good luck and prosperity. It represents the five elements of wood, earth, water, fire, and metal. Money Tree: The Money Tree is another popular plant that is said to bring wealth and prosperity. It has a braided trunk and is often planted in a container filled with coins or other symbols of wealth. Jade Plant: The Jade Plant is a succulent that brings prosperity and good fortune. It is often placed in the wealth area of a space, such as a corner of the living room or home office. Ficus: The Ficus is a plant that is understood to bring positive energy and prosperity. It is often placed near a window or entryway to help circulate positive energy throughout the space.

- Declutter: A cluttered living room can block the flow of energy and create stress. Keep the room tidy and organized by getting rid of unnecessary items.

- Furniture Placement: The placement of furniture plays a vital role in creating a harmonious living room. The sofa should be placed against a solid wall with a clear view of the entrance. Chairs and tables should be arranged in a way that promotes conversation and social interaction.

- Colour Scheme: Utilize your Astrological colours with wisdom.

- Lighting: Good lighting is essential for a harmonious living room. Use natural light as much as possible, and supplement with soft, warm lighting in the evenings.

- Art and Decor: Art and decor can be used to enhance the energy of a living room. Choose pieces that bring joy and positivity, and avoid anything that is negative or disturbing.

By following these guidelines, you can create a living room that promotes balance, harmony, and relaxation.

Lounge/Living room combined with Dining room

- First, it's important to create separate areas for the living room and dining room. Use rugs, lighting, or plants to define the spaces. This will help to avoid the energy from each area clashing and conflicting with each other.

- Next, consider the placement of the furniture. The living room furniture should be arranged in a way that promotes conversation and connection. Use a sofa and chairs to create a relaxing seating area and position them facing each other.

- When it comes to colour, utilize your Astrological colours.

- Finally, incorporate natural elements such as plants or flowers into the space to bring a sense of vitality and life. Adding artwork or decor that represents abundance, such as a bowl of fruit, can also enhance the energy in the room.

Lounge/Living room incorporating a child's toy area

The living room is often the centre of family life and can include a children's toy play area. When creating a Fung Shwa living room with a children's toy play area, it's important to consider the energy flow and organization of the space. First, decide a location for the play area that is away from the main entrance and not blocking the flow of energy into the room. Next, select furniture that is both functional and aesthetically pleasing. Use storage containers or baskets to organize toys and keep clutter to a minimum. Consider using a low shelf or cabinet with doors to keep toys hidden when not in use.

To balance the energy in the living room, incorporate natural elements such as plants, fresh flowers. Lastly, be mindful of the placement of electronics in the living room. Place the television and other electronics away from the play area to avoid over stimulation and create a more peaceful environment for play and relaxation.

Windows and Curtains

The windows in your house are reflective doorways into the Soul, so the same vibration of colour or tone in a room, should also be draped around the windows. By creating this effect, we are bringing harmony into the Soul consciousness of the room. Place your drapes on either side of a very large window to help frame the view that you are looking out on. It seems to be the fashion today to not have curtains on the windows; people are searching for white and light, so the next best thing is to place a plant with soft leaves to the right side of the window. This plant helps satisfy the emotions and takes away the nakedness of a bare window.

A White Room

If you leave everything white, you will lighten your energy – although, sometimes you lose your thoughts, too, so you need another colour to stimulate the senses of the mind and this can be achieved by utilizing your Astrological colour. White is a perfect room for stillness; it brings a feeling of tranquillity to the inner self. A white room is great for conversation, as everyone in the room begins as equals.

Staircase

What is the difference to the mind if the staircase is on the left or the right side of the wall? Answer: If it is on the right wall, you will feel lighter, as it is alerting your emotional action to elevate you upstairs. You can place a painting on the left wall and it can be light and airy. If your staircase is on the left-hand side, your ego takes you up the stairs; put a calming painting on the opposite wall to balance the energy. A landscape can harmonize the mind; if you prefer another subject, chose something with strong colours.

What does the energy do on a spiral staircase? Answer: I once had a home with a spiral staircase, I noticed that, by the time I got to the top of the stairs, I had forgotten what I went up to retrieve; I had to learn to focus on my intention. A spiral staircase acts like a funnel: It lifts us up, although I quickly came to realize, by the time we have walked up the staircase, the strategy of our thinking has altered.

Books

Books are considered to be a source of knowledge, inspiration, and personal growth. Here are some guidelines for arranging books:

- Declutter: Before arranging your books, go through them and declutter. Keep only the books that are meaningful to you and that you plan to read or reference in the future. Let go of any books that no longer serve a purpose in your life.

- Group by category: Group your books by category, such as fiction, non-fiction, self-help, biographies, etc. This makes it easier to find the book you need and also creates a sense of order.

- Use bookends: Bookends not only keep your books in place, but they can also add a decorative element to your bookshelf. Choose bookends that are sturdy and aesthetically pleasing.

- Avoid overcrowding: Don't pack your books too tightly on the shelf. This can create a feeling of overwhelm and chaos. Leave some breathing space between books to create a sense of calm.

- Arrange with intention: When placing your books on the shelf, think about the energy you want to create. For example, if you're looking for more inspiration in your life, place your favourite inspirational books front and centre.

- Keep books in good condition: Make sure your books are in good condition and free from dust and damage. This not only enhances the energy of your space, but it also shows respect for the knowledge and inspiration contained within the books.

Your Notes:

CHAPTER TEN

Fung Shwa Design—Adult Bedrooms

Be aware of what energy is overpowering you in your bedroom. Keep this room light and free; it does not need to be cluttered and crowded with furniture. This is the area where when you rest and sleep; it is where you have the opportunity to allow your light bodies, which are your Soul's veils – or, another term is "your personalities (aspects of self) that are in abeyance to you" – their time to stretch and travel around.

As previously stated, the complementary ideals of Fung Shwa are up, down, in, and out; so, through clarity and creating our colour, we seem to come to order to motivate and empower the self. We step "up" into a kitchen or bathroom. To calm the mind, we step "down" into a bedroom or family room. We step "in" to a study, library, or lounge room for seclusion, and we step "out" through the doorway onto the veranda or patio to broaden our horizons.

So, when stepping into the bedroom we must step "down", and that means that the floor should be of a slightly darker colour than the walls. We step down to use this room as the place where we come back home to self – that is, to achieve self-sanctification. Remember that the only reason we need to sleep is to rebalance our ego! It needs somewhere to relax. If we have a floor with a lighter colour than the walls, we feel extended beyond our belief! There is no achievement to balance our thoughts to prepare our body for sleep; we need to encapsulate the ego back into itself in order to harmonically balance the automatic responses of the nervous system. Sometimes the ego needs to be desired before it can go into a sleeping state, and white would put it off before it could even begin. Lethargic lovemaking needs to be stimulated. Maybe a strong vibrant colour would help to change one's mind. The colours that attract themselves to our sexual connotations are deep red, mauve, or chocolate-brown. These colours stimulate the senses into wanting to attract sexual satisfaction.

A few guidelines on using Fung Shwa in the bedroom for relaxation:

- Clear Clutter: The first step to creating a harmonious bedroom is to clear away any clutter. Clutter represents stagnant energy that can affect your sleep quality and overall energy level. Get rid of anything that is no longer needed or used in the bedroom, and organize what remains in a way that promotes relaxation and calmness.

- Balance the Bed: The bed is the most important piece of furniture in the bedroom and should be placed in a commanding position where you can see the door but not in direct line with it. This helps to create a sense of security and control in the room. Additionally, ensure that the bed is balanced with two nightstands, lamps, and pillows. This creates a sense of harmony and equality in the room.

- Decorate with your Astrological colours.

- Add Soft Lighting: Soft lighting is essential in creating a relaxing and peaceful bedroom. Use dimmer switches on overhead lights or add soft coloured globes.

- Lamps to create a warm and cosy atmosphere. Avoid harsh fluorescent lighting, as it can be too bright and stimulating.

- Incorporate Natural Elements: Crystals can help to balance the energy in the bedroom.

- Keep Electronics to a Minimum: Electronics such as TVs, computers, and cell phones emit electromagnetic radiation that can disrupt sleep patterns and affect energy levels. Keep these items to a minimum in the bedroom, and if possible, remove them altogether.

<u>Bed linen</u>

Choosing the right bed linen is an important aspect of creating a harmonious and balanced bedroom according to Fung Shwa. It is recommended to use high-quality natural fabrics, such as cotton or linen. Bed linen with busy or bold patterns should be avoided as they can create a sense of chaos and unrest. Additionally, it is recommended to have several sets of bed linen on rotation to ensure that they are frequently washed and refreshed.

Essential Oil for relaxation

There are several essential oils that can promote relaxation and a peaceful atmosphere in the bedroom. Some popular choices include lavender, or chamomile. Lavender is particularly well-known for its calming properties and is often used to promote better sleep. Chamomile has a soothing and calming effect. These essential oils can be used in a diffuser or added to a spray bottle with water to mist over the bedding before sleep.

How to make your own mister with a spray bottle using lavender oil. Making your own mister with a spray bottle using lavender oil is an easy and inexpensive way to freshen up your bedroom while promoting relaxation. First, you will need a spray bottle, preferably one made of glass to avoid any potential chemical reactions with the oil. Fill the bottle with water, leaving some room at the top for the essential oil. Add a few drops of high-quality lavender essential oil, about 10-15 drops for a standard spray bottle. Shake the bottle well to mix the oil with the water. You can adjust the amount of essential oil based on your preference. To use: simply shake the bottle and spray the mist around your bedroom, on your bed linens for a soothing and calming effect.

Windows/Curtains

The windows in your house are reflective doorways into the Soul, so the same vibration of colour or tone that is being draped on the bed, should also be draped around the windows. By creating this effect we are bringing harmony into the Soul consciousness of the bedroom. Place your drapes on either side of a very large window to help frame the view that you are looking out on. That frame represents a veil, where the bedroom does not run away from you; instead, the veil represents the unconscious/higher mind releasing itself back to you.

As stated previously, it appears to be a current trend to forgo curtains on windows. In such cases, I would recommend draping a piece of fabric across the top of the windows in a colour that matches your bedspread. Allow it to drape slightly down the left side of the window, as it pleases your ego that your window is not exposed to the elements. Metaphysically, this alerts you to the fact that there is a form of protection around you when you are asleep. If this does not suffice, the next best thing is to place a plant with soft leaves to the right side of the window. This plant helps satisfy the emotions and takes away the nakedness of a bare window. By the way, a large window in the bedroom symbolizes freedom, openness, and a readiness to receive all.

Your Notes:

CHAPTER ELEVEN

Fung Shwa Design—Children's Room

Do not choke the children's room with clutter and toys. Your child can only play with so many toys at one time. Put the rest away and periodically exchange the choice of toys, which gives them the time to reinvest in their own personal property, as this opens the doorway of their precious little minds which strikes a concordance of their inner selves. You will learn to understand which toys become a favourite with your child. And for goodness' sake, not too many colours – this keeps the child's mind activated and, on the go, all the time. Are you beginning to understand this dreaded discord (or dis-ease) that we have named "ADD"? These colours are reflecting through the child's sleep as well; these colours may be appealing to you, but too many colours will over activate the child's behavioural patterns. Your child is looking for a respite in his/her own domain. This room is supposed to be his/her inner sanctuary! Now, for the big one: By using a variety of colours, you are pleasing the excuses that you make when you are not emotionally in touch with your little ones – enough of this! Two colours are enough for them to cope with when they are young, if need be, use a third colour in a very limited amount to highlight and balance the colour spectrum, you are aiming for.

In your children's bedrooms, please promote their Astrological colours! Use these colours on their walls to remind them that they are a part of your family, but also individuals. A child is given a vibration that is required to harmonize the inner feelings with the outer; these are the building blocks of shaping their own personal character. Your children will soon begin to learn to release their own confirmation.

Be careful with the colour of yellow or lemon in your child's room, as this colour activates the mind very quickly. In other words, your child can exhibit erratic behaviour at short notice. Your children already know that the colour of their rooms are compatible to their Soul energy. If children do not think that their parents are living up to their own expectations, those children think that they have the Divine right to autonomically test their parents' patience over and over again. As mentioned previously, please take note of the number of children with Attention Deficit Disorder (ADD) and Attention Deficit Hyperactivity Disorder (ADHD); this number has jumped to the top of the order throughout many countries' education systems.

Let me explain the previous paragraph again. Our children are also aware that, if parents are not living up to the requirements that they place on their children, those children will reject the outcome. The parents are trying to emphasize their own mistakes back to the children, through what the parents are not capable of accepting in regard to themselves. The children, in all their glory, will try to explain all this back to the parent, through telepathic announcement. Yellow – or lemon – is the colour of the sanctification from God/Collective Consciousness, and children will do their utmost to gain attention and to release their own frustrations.

A few guidelines on designing calming children's bedroom:

- Design the bedroom using the child's Astrological colour using wisdom.

- Use natural materials: Furnishings made from natural materials such as wood, cotton, and wool can help create a more harmonious and grounded space. Avoid synthetic materials as they can emit harmful chemicals.

- Avoid clutter: A cluttered space can create chaos and stress, especially for children. Encourage your child to keep their room tidy by providing ample storage space and organizing systems.

- Position the bed correctly.

- Add a grounding element: Earthy elements such as plants or crystals can help ground the energy in a child's bedroom, promoting a sense of stability and security.

- Avoid harsh lighting: Bright, harsh lighting can be overwhelming for children. Use soft, diffused lighting to create a cosy and inviting atmosphere.

- Incorporate meaningful artwork: Choose artwork that reflects your child's personality and interests. This can help create a sense of identity and personal empowerment.
- Rose Quartz is a beautiful pink crystal that is associated with love, compassion, and emotional healing for self. Placing Rose Quartz in a child's room can help to promote a loving and nurturing environment, and provide several benefits to the child.

Bed linen

Choosing the right bed linen is an important aspect of creating a harmonious and balanced bedroom according to Fung Shwa. It is recommended to use high-quality natural fabrics, such as cotton or linen. Bed linen with busy or bold patterns should be avoided as they can create a sense of chaos and unrest. Please wait until the child gets older. Additionally, it is recommended to have several sets of bed linen on rotation to ensure that they are frequently washed and refreshed.

Your Notes:

CHAPTER TWELVE

Fung Shwa And Relationships—The Compatibility Of The Personal Colours

When you form a relationship with a life partner, that relationship should be equal and balanced in order for it to succeed. We create that equality through giving and receiving. If the relationship is not equal, and one partner sacrifices his/her life for the other, problems will begin, and the relationship will need to be brought to attention every day.

Watch how your relationship has the chance to expand and grow when you decorate your home in the colours that are appropriate for each of you.

You birthed onto the planet on a particular day and time, which created a sign of metaphoric form for you to follow (i.e., your Astrological wheel). Through Einstein's "Theories of Relativity", I connected to how the arching of space and time creates each colour and then brings it into the fields of Collective Consciousness. Colour is an added value to the harmonic conversion of the planet; it is a mental tool that is helping to connect you to one another. Each one of your signs has already attained its own colour, and those colours must collate compatibly in order to harmonize with your inner blueprint – this is the Alchemy produced through your unconscious/higher mind.

I had the pleasure of becoming an interior designer through many years of studying the energy ley lines that assist with our human potentiality. When my mind became enhanced with this wisdom, I found that I could shift the possibilities of how to communicate with a couple aiming for compatibility in their relationship towards one another. This proved to have a great success rate.

I use my energy through the hearts and minds of those who share the homes that I enter. My job is to place light and harmony into that home, and I accomplish that through using the compatibility of the personal colours that each occupant is here to achieve.

Please refer to the chapter titled "Your Astrological Colours" to discover the colours aligned with your astrological sign. As examples for now, we will consider the signs of Libra and Virgo.

Like most signs that follow one another, these two signs are not compatible energy by any means; one always expects from the other, and each walks away from the message given. They are both trying to cohabitate with one another; as in all signs, the responsibility is always left to one person or the other. In this relationship of earth (Virgo) and air (Libra), there will be a tussle of egos along the way. Libra must always keep the wind low, as blowing too heavily in this relationship will cause problems; when we blow earth (Virgo) into the air (Libra) it creates dust, and dust creates irritation.

The colours of Virgo are the darker shades of the earth; for Libra, they are the lighter colours of the air. That is the colour scheme that their house should align with. Through creating this scene, those colours will help combine both partners into a form of compatible energy, where one will learn to respect the other. It also stops arguments in the house!

We will begin with the bedroom, where we learn to bring an ease of compatibility into a closer union. When stepping into the bedroom we must step "down", and that means that the floor should be of a slightly darker colour than the walls. We step down to use this room as the place where we come back home to self – that is, to achieve self-sanctification. Remember that the only reason we need to sleep is to rebalance our ego! It needs somewhere to relax. If we have a floor with a lighter colour than the walls, we feel extended beyond our belief! There is no achievement to balance our thoughts to prepare our body for sleep; we need to encapsulate the ego back into itself in order to harmonically balance the automatic responses of our central nervous system.

For compatibility in this relationship, we need two colours, so we choose a deep olive green for Virgo and a pale sky blue for Libra. We now have to choose a third colour that will enhance through both of these colours. There are 480 shades of green and 480 shades of blue; by blending two of these colours with one of the other, we can create a choice of 1,440 colours. We can also use silver or gold to abbreviate or separate these colours. Silver represents the inner systems and also represents the transformations of the freedom of self-discovery. Grey and light blue are mutable with silver, which means that they are secondary colours. Gold is a different equation; it brings us back into the centre of the self, and it also empowers the psyche of the outer self. Gold condenses energy, and so its energy must be applied in a forthright manner. It is the focus of all, and I like to call it the "geometry of the mind". Silver is a question searching for an answer. On the other hand, gold is an answer searching for a question. Be careful with the use of gold in a room; keep it limited, as it has a direct energy and makes you live up to the thought in your moment. For compatibility to the mind, we use less gold than silver. Viewing the colour gold dehydrates the body, and it also tires you out very quickly. In the presence of the colour gold, your ego has difficulties keeping up with its own demands!

We come now to the kitchen, which must activate this partnership, so let's see how we can incorporate the Virgo and Libra vibration into it.

As stated in a previous chapter, we step "up" into a kitchen, so the floor should be of a lighter colour than the walls. That will make all the difference to the education/energy system of preparing a meal. Lots of stainless steel in the kitchen enhances the mind into a form of cleanliness, where, as we use the pots and pans, we want to clean them immediately. The reflection of the pots enhances the cooking, increasing the desire to make it be more modified, more exemplified; this, of course, creates the illusion that the meal is more palatable, and so we appreciate it more when we eat it.

We can choose three or four different shades of sky blue for the Libra, and three or four different shades of olive green for the Virgo. Light green is emotional; it affects the heart, so it can help to lighten the cooking. Blue is the colour of communication; you have greater difficulties expressing your truth when you are standing in a blue room, so bring in a neutral tone (e.g., a pastel tint), which will create a hint of lightness.

The Virgo and Libra combination should not paint their kitchen in yellow, as they would be turning themselves inside out; in other words, they would be reversing their own psyches. They would not move forward; but, instead, they would pull themselves back. We must try to separate their individual colours; so please blend and harmonize with a third colour.

We step "into" the lounge room – not "up" or "down" – and we are still using the appropriate shades of blues and greens. Your home is your pure energy; it is your light, wisdom, and knowledge, so we should extend the same tone throughout the house. We do not want this temple of yours to be so busy with colour that your mind is jumping from one subject to another, not knowing what to do or in which direction to flow. Try to create compatible colours throughout the house in order to create an energy flow through each doorway. Let the same colour flow through into every room. Do not ostracize one room against the other. It's your home; please allow it to form a sense of compatibility with your mind!

I have chosen to give you two difficult energies here – Libra and Virgo – to learn from and work with. The subtle differences that you create for yourself must ensure that the relationship works to benefit you and your partner.

The best choice always is a white interior, as you are automatically living in the unconscious (higher) clear energy, and the windows of success are always open to you.

I have had two cream-coloured houses, and I always felt low – not necessarily lonely or sad, but my energy felt low. I used to become so frustrated with trying to make those houses compatible to my way of thinking. To ease my frustration, I painted the interior of both houses in a soft white, where my mind was free to magnify my possibilities, to reign supreme. That change made all the difference!

CHAPTER THIRTEEN

Paintings And Pictures

Have you ever realized the volume of energy a painting or picture can consume in a room? Is it the right shape or size to create harmony in the room? Does it heighten the room, or does it make the room appear smaller? Does it make you feel happy or depressed? Paintings or pictures play an important role in each room. They are there to represent an illusion of your inner mind. That is why you have purchased it in the first place!

If you have a large room, you can hang a large painting on the wall; but, if so, please keep the wall free of other furniture, which allows the painting to make its own statement! Try to place it opposite a doorway where it is the first thing that one notices upon walking into the room. If you have a large painting, and the room is small, paint the wall a light pastel colour; chose one of the colours embedded in the painting, with a slightly darker shade of the same colour for the other walls in that room.

This will enhance the painting in the room, and others will notice the objective of contemporary design that you have set out to achieve. The lighter the colour, the more perspective that you are enhancing throughout the room. The painting begins to create its own volumes of design, and you will find that the Collective Energy will ensconce its way holographically around the room. You are creating a 3D effect, where you will participate with the painting! What are you accomplishing by having an elongated shape; does the room appear taller? Does having a large rectangle spread across the room appear to extend and widen the room? Every geometrical shape either adds or subtracts to the volume of space that you are walking into!

Your Notes:

CHAPTER FOURTEEN

Mirrors

Let's talk about mirrors. The mirror is an illusion; it reflects back to us the thought that we have in that moment. Sometimes we can look at our reflection in the mirror and know that we look good, but sometimes that illusion of self can really turn us off.

Self has an idea, and it thinks a thought; the left brain spends its whole life trying to over control the self, through the worldly realms of our ego. Remember therefore, that the illusion of who we are has to reflect back. It is the reflection of both the illusion and the self, viewing one another that allows the unconscious/higher mind to step in to validate the thought. You would be surprised at the number of consultations I have had with beautiful young people who claim they are ugly.

When we enter a bathroom, the mirror should be placed on the right side of the room. Why? We must turn our face in order to look through the right brain. This fortifies our thoughts and returns a strength that sometimes we do not feel when we first wake up to greet the dawn of a new day. We have just returned from visiting the land of the never-ending story; and, for some of you, it takes time to collect and gather your thoughts together, especially if you are caught up with an emotion that has not yet been disentangled or strengthened.

The ego also likes to be in control of us every minute of our day; so, if the mirror is on the left side of the room, its confidence can build itself up to make us automatically want to control others. Why? We have not regained our own composure through balancing our mind to begin our day at this time. It's the little things that we sometimes forget.

The recommended colour to paint the walls of the bathroom would be bright with white. White serves the purpose of activating the mind for the day ahead. Lemon, in particular, automatically induces quick mental focus. The colour blue helps prepare the mind for future conversations and interactions that will be encountered throughout the day.

During consultations with my clients, I often inquire about their occupational roles. This information assists me in understanding the intellectual confrontations they face each morning. Interestingly, I discovered a correlation: the higher the position they fulfilled, the more predominant the use of white in their bathroom décor had to become. Why white? This colour automatically prepares their mind and aligns them to uphold their leadership position within the company or business enterprise. It sets their mind into its royal acclaim and they can enter their office with the right mindset.

Beige – or other light, sandy colours – we find that this colour is not always applicable to the early morning mind; those colours certainly benefit us more in the evening, when we are ready to collapse into bed. These colours also hold us back into yesterday's thinking, which creates an opening for the next excuse to birth at the beginning of the next day.

A section of my training through Shamanism was to find out how many mirrors were in a house, in what position those mirrors were situated in each room, and whether they were in the bedroom and bathroom. That task was done in order for me to register how the emotions of the occupants gathered and prepared them for their day. I learned how to predict whether they would have a good or a bad day, depending on how they faced themselves early in the morning.

Some final thoughts on mirrors. A mirror at the end of a hallway is appropriate for helping the illusion to correct its own behaviour when walking in a confined space. A mirror at the end of each level of a staircase helps a person who is tired at the end of the day to find his/her strength to walk up or down the stairs.

Your Notes:

CHAPTER FIFTEEN

Fung Shwa And The Bathroom

Fung Shwa is not limited to just the common areas of a home. It also extends to bathrooms. A bathroom is a place where we clean and refresh ourselves, and the energy or chi in a bathroom should be pure and clean to promote good health and well-being.

As previously stated in Chapter Fourteen, the recommended colour to paint the walls of the bathroom would be bright with white. White serves the purpose of activating the mind for the day ahead. Lemon, in particular, automatically induces quick mental focus. The colour blue helps prepare the mind for future conversations and interactions that will be encountered throughout the day.

During consultations with my clients, I often inquire about their occupational roles. This information assists me in understanding the intellectual confrontations they face each morning. Interestingly, I discovered a correlation: the higher the position they fulfilled, the more predominant the use of white in their bathroom décor had to become. Why white? This colour automatically prepares their mind and aligns them to uphold their leadership position within the company or business enterprise. It sets their mind into its royal acclaim and they can enter their office with the right mindset.

When we enter a bathroom, the mirror should be placed on the right side of the room. Why? We must turn our face in order to look through the right brain. This fortifies our thoughts and returns a strength that sometimes we do not feel when we first wake up to greet the dawn of a new day. We have just returned from visiting the land of the never-ending story; and, for some of you, it takes time to collect and gather your thoughts together, especially if you are caught up with an emotion that has not yet been disentangled or strengthened.

The ego also likes to be in control of us every minute of our day; so, if the mirror is on the left side of the room, its confidence can build itself up to make us automatically want to control others. Why? We have not regained our own composure through balancing our mind to begin our day at this time. It's the little things that we sometimes forget.

Further guidelines on how to Fung Shwa a bathroom:

- Keep the bathroom clean, well-lit and ventilated: A clean, well-lit and ventilated bathroom creates positive energy and promotes a feeling of calmness and relaxation.
- Use your Astrological colours for accents and towel colours.
- Keep the toilet lid closed: Keeping the toilet lid closed helps to prevent the loss of energy and wealth, which can flow away through the open toilet, plus sanitary when flushing the toilet.
- Add plants: Plants are known to purify the air, and they also add life and vibrancy to the bathroom. Plants such as bamboo and orchids are great choices for a bathroom.
- Rounded edges for mirrors: Curves are ideal for creating a soft and inviting atmosphere.
- Use natural materials: Natural materials such as wood, stone, and bamboo are great for creating a calming and soothing atmosphere. Avoid synthetic materials, which can create a cold and sterile environment.

Your Notes:

CHAPTER SIXTEEN

The Laundry Room

The laundry room is an important part of the house. It is a place where we wash our clothes and cleanse the dirt and grime of the day. By creating a harmonious laundry room, we can bring positive energy into our homes and lives. Here are some guidelines for your laundry room:

- Keep the laundry room clean and clutter-free. A clean and organized laundry room will help to keep the energy flowing smoothly. Remove any items that are not related to laundry, and keep laundry supplies neatly stored away.

- Use your Astrological colours as accents. Good lighting will help to energize the space and create a welcoming atmosphere.

- Add plants. Plants help to purify the air and bring life energy into the space. Choose plants that are easy to care for and that thrive in low-light conditions, such as spider plants or peace lilies.

- Place crystals in the room. Crystals can help to purify the energy of the space and enhance the flow of positive energy. Place crystals in areas where they will catch the light and reflect it around the room.

- Place a mirror in the room. A mirror can help to reflect light and energy around the room, making the space feel larger and more open.

By following these summary guide-lines you can create a harmonious and inviting laundry room that will help to bring positive energy into your home and life.

Your Notes:

CHAPTER SEVENTEEN

The Garage

Fung Shwa can be applied to all areas of your home, including your garage. The garage is an important space for many people as it serves as a storage area for their vehicles, tools, and other equipment. By applying the following guide-lines you can create a more harmonious and positive energy flow that can help you achieve your goals and bring more prosperity into your life.

To Fung Shwa your garage, the first step is to declutter and organize the space. Get rid of anything that you don't need or use anymore, and make sure that everything has its place. This will create a more positive energy flow in the garage and make it easier for you to find what you need when you need it.

Next, pay attention to the lighting in your garage. If the space is dark and gloomy, it can create negative energy that can affect your mood and productivity. Consider adding more lighting to your garage, such as overhead lights, task lighting, or even a small lamp.

Another important aspect of garage Fung Shwa is the positioning of your vehicles. Make sure that your cars are parked in a way that allows for easy movement and flow in the space. If you have multiple cars, try to park them in a way that allows for a clear pathway between them.

In addition to the positioning of your vehicles, pay attention to the placement of any equipment or tools in the garage. Try to keep them organized and stored away when not in use, and make sure that they are easily accessible when you need them.

The car

- Clean and declutter: Keep the car clean and free from clutter. Remove any unnecessary items that don't serve a purpose.

- Scent: Use essential oils or air fresheners that have a calming and uplifting scent to create a positive energy flow within the car. Remember the smell of pine trees are invigorating and keep the mind refreshed, your concentration is foremost in attendance, where you pay a detailed attention to what you are momentary doing.

Your Notes:

CHAPTER EIGHTEEN

Place The Garden Inside The House And The House Inside The Garden

Interior and exterior designing is one of my great pleasures. I like to place the garden inside the house, and the house inside the garden. When the two work together, we have created the illusion of a broader perspective and also have doubled the space. The conversation is then free to roam around the room.

How many of you plan, from inside each window of your home, the view you would like to focus on outside? So many of you plan the exterior from outside! But, by looking through the windows and harmonizing with the outside, we have the opportunity to double the size of a small room and also bring in the colours from the view outside to complement the interior. I like to form a different picture outside each window, so that each room has its own respect, serenity, balance, and pleasure. Each room is a parallel world that is available for you to walk into at any time, but each serves its own unique purpose. A bedroom is to sleep in; a kitchen is to eat in; a lounge room is to relax in, etc.

If you have a view with a distant landscape, chose the paint for your room from the colours in the distance, but select softer, subtler tones of those colours for the paint. This will also extend the light in, and double the width of the room.

If you live in the suburbs and have a building right next door, please choose flowers or shrubs to be placed outside in the garden, and make sure that they are the same colour as your indoor walls and fabrics, as this will also extend the shape of the room. Another additive, which will create the illusion of space outside where you have a small room with a small window, is to plant your shrubs in a triangle, with the tallest shrub centred in the window when viewed from inside and the smaller shrubs placed on either side. This creates the illusion of making the window appear larger than it really is. A mirror placed opposite the window will enhance the view from outside allow more light in the room, and create an illusion of more interior space.

Your Notes:

CHAPTER NINETEEN

Fung Shwa Your House And Garden

The complementary ideals of Fung Shwa are up, down, in, and out; we step "out" through the doorway onto the veranda or patio to broaden our horizons.

Let us look now at the Chinese Compass of Influence, which changes with every author who realizes his/her own influence, according to the compatibility achieved through his/her information. The majority says that when we walk into a house, we have the four directions of North, South, East, and West.

North: Influences our career and business opportunities.

South: Influences our conversation, where the understanding of what we are creating is clarified.

East: Is associated with family and creativity, which is the bringing together of the family.

West: Is for the baptism of personal growth.

Look at your house now and decide what it is that you want to attract. How is it situated, and in what direction does it face? Where does one begin? Is the house for the beauty of those who live in it? Or is it for the people who have come to admire it? You would be amazed at how many of you chose the latter! You can have both when you take the time to prepare your mind before you begin. Your home represents your thinking realms; it becomes your temple. The result of that thinking creates your future success, so let's get your energy flowing in the right direction.

We look at what we want our visitors to think about as they walk from the gate to the front door of our house. It is the introduction we give to others that determines how long they stay, whether they would like to stay awhile, and how they wish to converse with us inside our temple, that we have named our home. The walk from the gate to the door creates the first important step. It does not matter whether the path is 2 or 200 meters long. Do not block people off at the gate before you have had the opportunity to walk them up to the front door.

Try not to create a straight pathway to the door, as there is no emotion created in a straight line; by creating an arch, or a curve, you will open up their emotional mind. Thank goodness the old designs of architecture are changing. A straight pathway announces to others that you are in your own control factor, and that this is really not a place where visitors should prolong a visit. Nothing can be attracted to, or created for, us through a straight line. Make yourself interesting to those who wish to search for you; become their mystery.

If you already have a straight pathway to the house, then your house will have less energy for freedom of conversation; the energy will come in the front door, go out the back, and you will have missed it! By announcing a curve in your pathway, you will autonomically change the internal energy of the house. This will also create a chance for your mind to bend with the energy, where you can create a dance through the art of conversation. Everyone is happy!

If the process to change the curvature of the pathway is difficult, create a flow of movable energy in the form of a water feature to the right of the path towards the house. Visitors will benefit from the placement of a small tree or collection of rocks to the left of their walk to your front door. Water is calming; it is a mirror reflecting an image of the inner self. These small introductions on the pathway create a pause in the mind; this always adjusts your visitors' thoughts before they knock on your door. When your visitors read this message, their unconscious mind subtly introduces them into a more passive approach before they connect to you.

You can lengthen the visitors' interest on a longer pathway through the water feature – or symbolic expression – which can be created closer to the house. It does not have to be large; you will attract a different vibration towards future conversations if there is movement in the water. Do you recall the beauty in the art of bonsai? Maybe you envisage a larger block of land in the future, where you have images of how you would like to plan the land. This can also be replicated in a normal house block, just on a smaller scale.

If the gate is directly in front of the door and the pathway is straight, try to take the rigidness out of the line; we can instigate the visitors' thinking automatically, up into their unconscious mind, where they begin to relax. Through the placement of the shrubs or plants, you can "widen" the pathway; by spreading out plants as you reach the front door, you will make the doorway appear wider. Whilst living in Europe amongst the ginger bread shaped houses, they appeared to be the same all the way down the street. When I was asked to exterior design the garden of one of the houses to make it appear different from the others, we added a small weeping tree and climbing vines of wisteria, to soften the approach of the entrance. The results were impressive, and the owners of another four houses asked me to do the same for them. Within two years, it had changed the outlook and culture of the whole street!

If you place a symbol on the left-hand side of the pathway and also want to place a water feature on the right-hand side of it, please be aware of how the energy of both will want to attract their own personalities, and each will diffuse the other. Stagger the mathematics; place the symbol before the water. The way to create this is to measure your pathway from the gate to the door and divide it into thirds if it is long or half the length of the pathway if it is shorter. For a smaller pathway, have one symbol near the gate on the left hand side of the path and a water feature or weeping shrub up closer to the door on the right hand side.

The first symbol of the pathway is devoted to the left-hand side of the pathway, and it is this area where we place three rocks – or we can begin with two stones of different height and a flat one in front; the smaller of the two larger ones are placed one in front of the other taller one, and the flat one is in front of both, in other words three different heights. They react unconsciously like a set of steps. Your visitors are initiated into a new experience of sensing an inner security;

if one feels secure, the emotional aspect of self is relaxed to where it is guided unconsciously into the relationship of the right brain. This section is placed farther away from the path, and, as your friends or visitors continue to walk up to the door, they are magnetically attracted to it.

With new housing estates the footpath is now the driveway with a small pathway leading to the front door, therefore the area is limited to a garden space between the path and the front of the house, which would not suffice this plan that I am explaining. We could place a weeping shrub in place of the stones on the way to the door, as this is a sense of approval coming from the owner to the guest that they are welcome. This is the first attraction, which unconsciously alerts the visitor to whose home they are entering into. These small idiosyncrasies create your character, and determine how your visitors are subconsciously preparing themselves to meet you. Allow your Fung Shwa to work on both your own and their behalf.

Occupants who have a slight curve in the pathway have the warp of the sun or light – or strength and emotions – so they have the gift of being able to create and warp their own subtle energies. Again, I would like to take this example further. If your path veers to the right, then we realize that this is the pathway of the sun. If it veers to the left, then it is in relationship to the moon. Sun and rock, moon and water, all bringing your elements into harmonizing with one another.

If you do not want to add water, your element of attraction can be a shrub or small weeping tree and this will also set the stage for the visitors' unconscious/higher mind to harmonize their ego. As visitors entering the home of someone else, a curve in the pathway changes our mind; so, by the time we open the door, it makes us more amenable to the mind of the owner, as we allow the unconscious mind to work on our behalf.

If you are placing a light on the pathway, make sure that it is on the right-hand side of the pathway. This, again, changes the consciousness of the people walking up to the front door, where they must learn to trust their fear!

As a visitor to this house, the garden you are entering will alert you to whether the owner wants to enjoy the company of conversation or be left alone. When you look at a house, you are looking at an inner reflection of the owner. Gardens give the person walking by an interpretation of the people living in that house; by creating a curved openness in your garden, your intelligence is shining through.

As occupants, we can learn to appreciate the thoughts of the people we would like to attract into our home, through the illusion we wish to relay back to them.

If you create a good design that has movement, you will automatically attract good energy into the home. People must walk up your pathway step by step; they are then given the opportunity to release their tension as they approach your front door.

More and more of you are running your businesses from home; it saves on overhead and allows you to devote more time to sanctifying what you wish to accomplish for yourselves. When someone rings your doorbell, you want him/her to want to walk in and feel confident in regard to what you have to offer. That makes the business transaction more personal.

I recently designed a garden in Warsaw, Poland. The owners had people trying to break into their house many times. Their garden was in a shambles; it was an open book to anyone passing by. This disorder also represented their mind. Over the next month, we placed a design together where everything registered with and through the unconscious recognition of the mind. It became very interesting and attractive to passers-by; many of them stood outside the yard, as they wanted to copy the structure we had created. To this day, no more intrusions have occurred.

By the way, wind chimes are used as a cure to help adjust the flow of energy, or Chi, in a space. Wind chimes produce a calming and harmonious sound that can help to counteract negative or stagnant energy. When the wind blows, the chimes move and produce a sound that helps to activate the Chi in the surrounding area. Wind chimes are often used to help create a sense of peace and tranquillity in a space, and they can also be used to protect against negative energy or bad luck. The specific type, size, and placement of wind chimes can vary depending on the specific needs and goals of the individual or space.

Your Notes:

CHAPTER TWENTY

Planting Trees In The Garden

When planting trees in the garden, remember that we are symbolically stepping up in order to metaphysically create a pyramid (or triangle structure) to face the front door; therefore, we must plant smaller trees at the front of the garden. I am talking here about the average house block, not acreage. It is the same with any energy: We start off small to create that which will become large.

A border of high trees around the fence line of a house unconsciously says, "Keep out! This is my territory!" Thus, we know that the owner of that property wants seclusion. If smaller trees are planted around the fence line, gradually opening up the area in front of the house, we begin to notice that we are looking into the house, not at it. This transference of energy tells the visitor, "This house is my castle." The house has to be high at the front to accommodate that design; if it is not, plant just one medium tree near the house, preferably on the left-hand side to represent your personal growth.

If you want to plant a tree, or if you already have trees, look to the root system to see what that tree represents about you. Some trees cannot grow a taproot, as they do not have enough strength in their inner core. That type of tree develops a shallow root system; it creeps and crawls just under the surface of the earth, representing a lazy species and also signifying a lack of inner strength in the property owner. The wind has control over this tree.

Trees that have taproots are very strong; they are stubborn old trees that just stand without moving and hold fast to the ground – for many of us, this also creates a sense of security, and we feel protected. Let me explain some different examples of trees.

The fichus tree is a solid protector that represents its own Collective Consciousness, where it can repeat itself over again. In its stubbornness to hold itself in the ground, the roots of the fichus become stronger; when its branches become too heavy, some species of this tree send trailer roots down from the branches to help support and strengthen it, alleviating some of its heaviness. Other types of fichus have root systems that come up out of the ground, and these make wonderful shady seats on a hot day. You will need a larger property for this type of tree, as they are so grand that they take up most of the yard; they also make fantastic tree houses for children.

When someone buys a house that has big old stubborn trees on it, they feel protected by those trees. These people were drawn to that house through the unconscious/higher mind, which said, "Here you are; this is suitable for you." The conscious energy relaxes enough to let these individuals know that they don't have to change their lifestyle, as the trees will protect them from the excuses that they make in their-day to-day life.

The poplar stands tall and narrow. It sheds it leaves, which means that it does not hang onto the past. Its trunk (spine) is always aligned, and this keeps us in touch with our own royal behaviour. We notice that the poplar is planted in groves entering into cities where the government of that country rules. These trees are informing those entering the city that this area does not make excuses for the people in it – or for anyone else.

Every type of tree is unique in what it represents. The giant redwood represents strength. The apple tree is a blessing for self. Palm trees represent our action. Bamboo has an amazing energy that helps our spine. Weeping trees remind us of our stages of surrendering to self, which awakens the Buddha energy – or alerts our Christ consciousness – that we are still in touch with ourselves.

Therefore, when we are planning a new garden, we are enquiring of self as to which plants we need for this new home, so that our family can grow mentally, physically, and spiritually. We should begin to plan how we can evolve through choosing plants that will complement our self; that is, as to how this garden can work with us and not keep us fixed in our old repetitive ways of thinking. We each may have certain plants that attract our attention; if you have this experience with any plants, make sure these are on your list to include in your garden! Why? Their essence is calling you unconsciously, seeking to replace in you what you are lacking in your own thoughts. Watch how the birds drop their seeds of the rain forest when your emotions are running dry, etc.

When we enter into a nursery to buy a plant, most of us don't look at the plant itself, we look at the colour or texture of its leaves; on a conscious level, we first notice the outer dimensions of the plant. All your Higher Self to walk into the nursery before your ego so that you can choose the right plants – that is, the plants which will be of service to you. If you ask the Universe what you need for yourself, you will automatically be led to the plants that you need to buy, not the plants that you think "just look pretty".

When you only see the prettiness of plants, you are using that as an excuse for the moment. It eases the emotions of the moment; it does not fix or dissolve the problem that is surrounding you. Plants have an emotion that correlates to what you are refusing to give to yourself.

Whilst in China recently, I spent many a day in their magnificent bonsai gardens, which I found quite pleasant and calming, as I found my inner peace in these sacred places. Those gardens seemed to bring me into their world as they came into mine; we became equal in thought. My stress of the day released itself when I could feel and sense this outer beauty. Most of the trees were hundreds of years old – and some were over a thousand years old – yet all of them were still alive, thriving in a flat, 8-inch tray.

In amazement, I watched the gardeners who had worked there all their lives. As they tenderly touched each tree, they talked to and caressed it, gently snipping the leaves. The majority of these gardeners were well into their eighties and had worked in this same place since they were small children. One man, who was a master gardener, had worked in the same position for more than ninety years, having begun as a four-year-old child. Imagine all the wisdom that these gardeners had gathered through spending their life supporting these trees, tending them and keeping them in an upright position, year after year. The trees must have felt tremendously loved, and the gardeners must have felt the trees' love release to them.

The Master Gardener

I would like to share a story with you; this is about a day in China that I will never forget. While walking through the avenues of the bonsai gardens with my guide, Chen, I had the pleasure of meeting the master gardener. (It is interesting to note that the Chinese, like the Aborigines, address you by your surname. Why is this so? Both cultures have already evolved up into the Divine language of the unconscious/higher mind!) Back to the story! This master gardener had been working as a caretaker in the same beautiful garden for more than ninety years. He began his apprenticeship at four years of age. In all of those years, he had never taken a day off from his work; he explained to me that he had a responsibility to his "children" – which were these magnificent trees – as they were beings lesser than he, and so he must nurture them so that they could find their own strength. He taught them how to talk to him, and he encouraged the stimulation of their mind, through tipping and pruning their branches twice a year – once in the spring to prepare them for the summer, and once in autumn to help them prepare for the winter, as this stimulated and educated their life force. In regard to humanity; we must also turn and face ourselves at these same times each year and are termed "turning points".

It took a period of twenty-eight years for this master gardener to finalize his apprenticeship, after which time, he could take full responsibility for his work and not have to rely on others' judgement. His training was the same as his own master's had been. He had promised the trees that he would be there for them, that he would talk with them and share their responsibilities. Some of these trees were many hundreds of years old, and yet they still survived in these small clay bowls.

As I looked into his magnificent eyes, he related his stories to me, all the while gently touching the old tree that he was working with. This tree was the oldest in the gardens; it had only the shell of its trunk remaining, with one small branch that had five leaves poking out at the top. According to its chart, this tree was around 1,100 years old. My heart shattered into a thousand pieces at the love that poured from him as he spoke his words. His own family had come and gone, and he was all that was left, so now he could devote the rest of his life to attending to his Spiritual family. My goodness! I could see how his strength had released through his power coming together in order for him to achieve his self-acclaim.

I did not want to walk away and leave this beautiful man; I realized that I was in the presence of wisdom. As I bowed to him and brought my hands together, I blessed him and thanked him for his time.

Chen and I walked away, and, as I dried the tears from my eyes, I felt ever so humble. Chen's arm slipped through mine, as I was teetering along the path, and he said, "Let's go on to the teahouse and have a small pause." As we walked along, I listened to Chen humming to himself, and I noticed that he would repeat the same sound over and over again. I asked if the song was an old one, and he smiled at me, saying, "No, it is not. It is I, calling myself back into harmony. Some of my 10,000 personalities (aspects of self/thoughts) need attention, but they are of no consequence in this moment, so I am informing them that we will share with one another at a later time.". My heart melted when I heard his words. How precious to be able to communicate so honestly with the self! What an easy way to be in control, to de-stress, and to release the pressure of the mind—all at the same time! It is so simple, isn't it? We Westerners still have such a long road to travel!

Turning Point: Through our allotted time, a self-awakening (review) automatically happens twice a year. In March through to April – it is known as the "Ides of March". One must turn around and face up to the responsibility of oneself! Again, it occurs in mid-August through to September, when it is known as the "Winds of Change". Through the Laws of Shamanism, we refer to both of these stages as the "Turning Point". Every human has the opportunity to turn and face themselves (metaphorically); once after our summer months, and once after the winter, to review our life and face up to the responsibilities of self that we have forced ourselves to overlook. (By the way, through the interpretation of the Greek and Roman myths, the "Ides of March" was known as a day of infamy through the assassination of Julius Caesar).

Your Notes:

CHAPTER TWENTY ONE

Plants

Fung Shwa is about how your mind coincides with the mind of the planet; it is where you work with other species that create the foundation of your DNA. Your DNA works with the evolution of the planet, and, as you become stronger within, it sets the scene for you to become more collected intellectually in the mind. That growth creates more action in your life, giving you the opportunity for your inner growth to work in a relationship with your inner nature – that is, the essence of you. "Nature" is another name for our Oracle, which, when brought up into the science of the mind, is representing the aura of our cells. It is here to supplement us by giving us what we are lacking through the innocence of our fear (ego) not knowing how to accept and understand our self.

Trust yourself enough to take the plants that your Higher Self has directed you to take. Take them home and say, "Okay, work with me; help me resurrect my old ways in order to allow for future change to come to me." You are surrendering to self, so those plants will then begin to supplement your weaker thoughts and realign you. It is like a big dose of antibiotics – or homeopathy, depending upon your preference – and it all works through the codes of mathematics, through all that is.

I once had a group of Cordyline plants at the front door of my house; as I faced the front door, these plants were on the left-hand side. My Higher Self planted that garden; I did not! Those plants represented my boredom with life, and they could sense my inner urge of wanting to further my education. By having those plants where they were, I was telling visitors that I wished to become an added value to myself; although, I still required advancement through more education.

Had I known the lesson from those plants at that time, I could have just agreed with them; as I walked out my door, with the Cordylines on my right side, I walked straight past and ignored them. My work schedule at that time did not allow the time for me to hear or see what they were expressing to me. When I went out the front door, I was working for the family, not on behalf of the family.

The Cordyline has long, narrow leaves that go straight up, so it was telling me to continue straight up with my thought of wanting to further my studies. In time, the plants overtook my thinking, and I signed up for an education at my local Collage to study social sciences. Your life is a game of the subconscious converting the conscious, which allows the unconscious (higher) realm to place itself in the middle of the other two; through your enquiring mind, the unconscious thus becomes available to teach both other realms (i.e., subconscious and conscious).

The fishbone fern represents the spine. When you are led to buy one of these plants, your Higher Self is directing you to straighten up your spine – that is, to lift up your consciousness and collect your personalities together. That fern also looks like a caterpillar, so your Higher Self is saying, "Come on now, lift yourself up! Transformation is on its way."

In Australia, we have a "hen and chicken" fern. The main plant is the "hen"; its fibrous roots hang outside the pot and send out many other little ferns that we call "chickens". Those chickens represent all our new thoughts, and the hen must make sure that the nourishment is supplied to them. If you receive one of those ferns as a gift, look at what your many thoughts are pronouncing to others – you are losing sight of self through martyring to others. In the old days, this plant was presented to the young bride to make her aware that her marriage was her preparation for pregnancy.

The shrub that contains a strong essence of perfume is planted outside your bedroom window; this allows the perfume to waft in during the night, which repairs the sexual body and also enhances your dreams. Those plants release their energy at night; they reconnect you back into the depths of your sexual zones to release the build-up of tension that you have consciously created in your mind. Through the perfume, your dreams have the opportunity to relax, where the mathematics can heal sections of your body that you quite simply ignore.

CHAPTER TWENTY TWO

Fung Shwa—Selling Your House

Selling a house can be a stressful and time-consuming process. However, using Fung Shwa can help attract the right energy to make the selling process more seamless. Here are some guidelines to help sell your house:

- Clear the Clutter: One of the most essential steps in selling your house is to declutter it. A cluttered house can create stagnant energy that will turn off potential buyers. Before putting your house on the market, go through each room and clear out any unnecessary items. Consider donating, selling or throwing away anything that does not serve a purpose or hold sentimental value.

- Create a Welcoming Entrance: The entrance of your house is the first thing potential buyers see. Therefore, it's essential to create a welcoming and inviting entrance. Make sure the pathway leading up to the entrance is clear and unobstructed. Add some plants, fresh flowers or a new doormat to make the entrance more inviting.

- Balance the Energy: Balance is the key and it is essential to create balance in your house before selling it. Start by placing furniture in a way that creates balance and flow in each room. Use colour to create a balanced and harmonious atmosphere. Avoid using too many dark colours, which can make the space feel heavy and overwhelming.

- Focus on the Kitchen and Bathrooms: The kitchen and bathrooms are two of the most important areas of the house. Ensure that they are clean, bright and uncluttered. Make any necessary repairs and upgrades to ensure they are in good working condition. Use fresh flowers or plants to add life to these spaces.

- Enhance the Curb Appeal: The outside of your house is just as important as the inside. Enhance the curb appeal by adding plants, flowers, and fresh paint. Make sure the lawn is trimmed, and any dead or dying trees or shrubs are removed.

- When it comes to selling a house, a person's life force plays an important role. If a person's life force is weak, it can create an energy imbalance that may make it difficult to sell the house. Therefore, it's important to ensure that the energy in the house is balanced and harmonious. It is also important for the seller to constantly visualise a sign with a banner of "Sold" across it. This sets the intention to the Universe/Collective Consciousness.

Your Notes:

CHAPTER TWENTY THREE

The Old Fashioned Ways

Excerpt from the book: "Decoding The Shaman Within", Chapter 1. My Maternal Grandmother Was An Alchemist, O.M. Kelly.

I remember that my grandmother had over one acre of garden around her house and as a child, I would walk with her as she gathered her flowers and herbs to decorate the table and her cooking was always exquisite to the pallet. For the setting on the breakfast table, we would have a vase of freshly cut herbs, which would release their essence to strengthen our thoughts for the day. These herbs were used in the forthcoming meals. Flowers were placed on the table in the evening and a mixture of herbs brushed into the floor and also on the carpet square with a damp straw broom which would crush the essence of the herbs to relax the mind after a busy day. These herbs were not allowed to be crushed until just after four o'clock in the afternoon, after the pressure lamps had been pricked and primed ready to serve us with light for the evening meal. Their essence could release and remove the odour of kerosene without overpowering the men when they took off their boots and hats and had scrubbed up in preparation for the evening meal after the end of a long day in the paddocks.

The garden was all coordinated and grandmother planted the colours according to the colours of the rainbow. Herbs were sprinkled throughout as a companion to the flowers. You were introduced into the white flowers when you walked outside the door, its colour cleared the cluttered mind and as you stepped forward you walked into the soft pinks; continuing down through the lilacs, into the blues of the cornflowers, then the greens which were the soft green of the Canterbury bells and onto the richer colours of lemons, oranges, reds and browns and as a child, it was like walking through a rainbow. My grandmother said that the colours were compatible with our inner alphabet as they urged us forward; our inner alphabet related to the words we would use, when we were busily thinking our thoughts. It was like an inner cleansing and healing of the chakras, as it is known today, back in my time it was known as Joseph's coat of many colours or the inner rainbow healing our self.

I knew how important each flower was by the colour they emitted from the plant. You could read the value of the flower and what it had to offer you by the strength of its colour. Even down to which part of the body it would be called to heal. The deeper the colour, the more it connected to the problem in the lower section of the body. The lighter the colour, the higher vibration was created. This is exactly the same as the colours we automatically release from our mind as we think each thought! We all have this inner rainbow that mathematically collects and arks its way up through our spinal column, when we think positive thoughts. These colours permeate their way throughout our aura, where they are reflected out to others.

Grandmother explained that the garden had much to teach us, as our body also worked on the same parallel as the garden. If we had thoughts that could not find their own strength, then there was a parasite that would create a nest for it to strengthen itself and a disease became immanent. My crops of vegetables were always successful. I learned to understand how the plant kingdom is identical to the human kingdom.

And we all know by now, that every species that has evolved on this planet, is indelibly imprinted and is mathematically registered within the genes of every human.

And in the centre of grandmother's land was the rose garden. There was a large rectangle green lawn, bordered with around a hundred rose bushes, all coordinated of course. We would pose for photos in the rose gallery, whether it was an engagement, Christmas gathering, wedding, anniversary or someone's birthday party. It did not matter if the weather was hot or cold, there was always a section of the garden that we could stand in front of and pose! That is the nice thing about my country, there is always a flower in bloom all year long. We saved the washing up water after the dishes were done, the bath water after we had finished our scrub up, the washing water when the clothes had been hung up to dry – all collected and bucketed out on to the garden. The men in the family did all of the preparation work to the soil and when the earth was ready, it was up to the women to put in the cuttings and strew the seeds.

We had our own meat from the chickens, turkeys, ducks, and geese; then there were the sheep, pigs, wild goats and cattle. We could supply our own terrines, brawns, casseroles, pickled and smoked meats, roasts, milk, cream, butter and cheese. We had our own hives, which supplied our honey and assisted us in making our own candles with ground up lavender heads to rest our mind throughout the night. We had soap that could be used throughout the day, and a different blend for the night wash.

We planted our own orchards for fruit, jams and preserves, vegetables to share with our meals and chutneys and relishes. We baked our own bread, cakes and biscuits from the harvest of the wheat, oats, rice, millet, maize, and barley that we harvested each year.

We made our soap mixed with oats and lavender and calendula for the women to replace the moisture in our skin. Grandmother's knowledge of Aromatherapy was amazing as she explained the use of flowers owing to her training in China. There was ground up barley and softly sieved sand for the men to lift the grease off their hands as they washed them. These gifts from the eternal kingdom served us in many different ways. There were six meals per day, three large and three smaller ones. No one became ill, as our mind had been forewarned with our herbal concoctions.

As the grapes that grew over the arbor at the rear of the house started to produce their new seasons growth, this helped keep the rooms cooler. Every child had to eat ten green grapes before they were ripe. This was to purify our blood and cleanse it after the short winter where we were rugged up all day. It worked! We were more than prepared for the long hot summer months ahead.

Grandmother never said "No! Don't touch." When I asked to rub a leaf together to emit the essence she would say, "yes, snip the fresh leaves cleanly from the top with your fingers, they are the freshest part of the plant and sniff the essence deep down into your lungs and anything nasty in the way of viruses, or pending diseases that is hanging around you looking for a place to reside and create itself, will soon leave home. Remember, we are all taught that God's gift to us is his garden." She also taught me how to plant my seeds with companion herbs. I learned the difference between herbs and weeds. A herb would benefit and a weed would hinder my flowers and vegetables. I learned to watch what weeds found their way forward into evolving their next evolutionary step, as they sprung up around my new seedlings, to see if they were a robber that would interfere with the energy of the new plant or if they were a friend which would form a relationship to strengthen the plant. The robber would feed itself on the innocence of the new growth; it was like a parasite and had to be removed.

To return back to the story, my grandmother taught me back in the late-forties through to the mid-fifties, where and how to attract energy through planting the dried cow horns which were filled with their own waste products and buried, then months later were taken out of the ground and buried in the new garden bed. She also liked some of the cow horns to be filled with fresh sea sand once a year. When we had killed the beast, the horns were severed and placed on top of the ant nests; which were built up into mounds behind the toilet and this was half way down the paddock and a good three-minute walk away. I often wondered why the meat ants had collected to build their nests behind there. Anyway, the ants would clean the fibrous tissue out of the horns. We also used the cow horns as beakers to drink out of; flower vases on the table or cupboard, and they were lovingly polished with bee's wax where they glowed through the lamp light on the table. It wasn't until the generators came out that we could enjoy the power of electricity with our 25-watt globes, which was only allowed for two hours of a night.

When members of the family would go for holidays to the ocean once a year after the wheat harvest, they had to bring back a fresh bucket of sand from the beach for grandmother. The silica and salt of the sand once buried inside the cow horns would change the molecular structure of the soil and no matter how tired or parched it felt, it would purify the soil and spring into life once again.

Grandmother having spent those three years in China in 1903-6, was taught how to hum to her vegetables and she would walk through her garden humming to her plants, which I now understand was creating a vibration firstly for the plants, as well as assisting her to reach her own resonance to promote her own sound. I can still recall how some of them seemed to bow to her as she walked down her rows. This fascinated me as there wasn't any wind to move them; they knew her sound and were honoring her.

We now understand that the symbol OM or AUM when chanted creates its own frequency, where we lift the eternal layers of consciousness to create a field of levitation which can occur, and my grandmother lived it around 140 years ago.

I can still recall the smell of the ocean when I put my head over the bucket as a child. It stayed fresh and never went sour and the smell was there all year long. There were millions of tiny little shells in the sand and these were ground up in the mortar and the pestle and grandmother would create them into a paste and this was scattered around certain plants who were not feeling too well. She explained to me that the shapes of these tiny shells were in perfect unison to God's original plan and that they would help to heal whatever they came into contact with. These old wives' tales are still used as a reflection of today's intuitiveness, as they were all chemically free and correct at that time of our evolution. Today we have continued on with their story and advanced upon the knowledge of the past. Their mathematical shape would release the correct prescription to the plant. Today we are more aware of the spiral the golden mean creates as reflected in a sea shell.

Once again it was the men's job to collect the sand, as they had to make sure that it was not spilt on the way home, which was just on nine hundred kilometers away, over rough dirt roads. One memory that still abounds in my mind is that I can recall the thrill of driving on a bitumen road. The car seemed to glide over the road and I often stuck my head out of the car window to see if the tires were really on the road. I felt like we were flying as I could not feel the bumps of the corrugated dirt roads!

Another teaching of grandmother's was how to coil a piece of copper pipe and plant it into the ground; the end of the pipe had to be planted six inches into the ground to transfer the energy around the vegetable beds. She placed three copper coils around the rows in a triangle shape. It could not be four; that didn't work as four would divert the energy and could cancel itself out. Needless to say, we were again reminded that God's gift to us was in his garden.

I loved the stories she told, especially in regards to the plant kingdom. That everything that God had designed had to earn its place on this planet. (Learning comes from explanations that we receive from someone else; earnings are released to us from your inner self). Every plant, every tree, all needed their own temperament to encourage them to grow, to advance themselves. They needed the minerals from under the earth and the elements in the earth to sustain them. Their territory became their boundary, they never ventured outside of their own perimeter, until the species of the planet assisted. Just as our own body needs the elements of the earth and minerals to keep us alive. Their seed could be carried along with the birds, the wind, the fire or the water, which propagated further down the track where they found a new home in soil of same mind. And that goes for every species on the planet as well; they and we, have all had to earn our own, and their place to exist on the earth.

I have been honored to have been brought up to have had the training from my grandmother to see the world from an inner perspective, where every species that has evolved before us, has been in preparation for us as human, to inherit their kingdoms, as I now know that the evolution of our brain is the mathematical make-up of every species, that has evolved for us to become responsible for ourselves.

CHAPTER TWENTY FOUR

Crystals And Cleansing A House Of Negative Energy

There are many books on crystals and the placement in the home. I have included a short over-view chapter on crystals.

Crystals have been used for centuries in many different cultures for their healing and spiritual properties. They are able to absorb, store, and transmit energy, making crystals an excellent tool for balancing and enhancing energy.

The ancient Egyptians were known for their use of crystals for both practical and spiritual purposes. They believed that certain crystals had healing and protective properties, and used them in various rituals and ceremonies. One of the most famous examples of the ancient Egyptians use of crystals is their use of Lapis Lazuli. This deep blue stone was highly prized for its beauty and was often used to create elaborate jewellery and decorative objects. Lapis Lazuli was also ground into a powder and used as a cosmetic, as it was believed to have healing properties for the skin. In addition to Lapis Lazuli, the ancient Egyptians also used other crystals, such as Carnelian, Amethyst, and Clear Quartz, for their healing properties. They believed that these crystals could be used to balance and align the body's energy centres, or chakras, and that they could help to ward off negative energy and promote emotional wellbeing. The ancient Egyptians also used crystals in their religious and spiritual practices. For example, Clear Quartz was often used to represent the power of the sun, while Amethyst was associated with the birthing of their children, also with the god Osiris. Crystals were sometimes carved into the shapes of sacred symbols or animals and used as talismans or amulets for protection and good luck.

Other cultures that used crystals:

Ancient Greeks: The ancient Greeks believed that Amethyst could prevent drunkenness and promote sobriety. They also believed that Citrine was associated with the god of the sun and that it could bring prosperity and abundance.

Chinese: The Chinese have a long history of using crystals for healing and spiritual purposes. Jade, for example, was highly prized for its beauty and believed to have powerful healing properties for the kidneys and liver. They also used crystals like Quartz and Jade to balance and harmonize the body's energy.

Native Americans: Many Native American tribes believed that crystals had the power to heal both the body and the spirit. They used crystals like Turquoise, Jasper, and Obsidian in their jewellery and sacred objects, and believed that each crystal had its own unique energy and symbolism.

Hinduism: In Hinduism, crystals like Clear Quartz and Amethyst are believed to be associated with different deities and can be used in various spiritual practices, such as meditation and prayer.

Overall, the use of crystals has been a common thread throughout many different cultures and civilizations throughout history. Today, people continue to explore the potential of crystals for healing, spirituality, and personal growth.

Let us explore some of the most popular crystals and their properties that you can use in your house.

- Clear Quartz: Clear Quartz is known as one of the most versatile crystals. It amplifies energy and brings clarity and highlights all the good energy in the room. Clear Quartz can be used to enhance the energy of other crystals and to balance the energy in a room. Place a clear quartz cluster in your living room to promote a peaceful and harmonious environment.
- Amethyst: Amethyst is a beautiful purple crystal that is associated with spirituality and intuition. It promotes a sense of calm and relaxation, making it an excellent crystal for the bedroom. Amethyst can also be used to promote mental clarity and focus, making it a great addition to a home office or study.

- Rose Quartz: Rose Quartz is a soft pink crystal that is associated with love and compassion. It promotes emotional healing and attracts love and positive relationships. Place a piece of Rose Quartz in your bedroom or living room to promote a loving and peaceful environment.

- Black Tourmaline: Black Tourmaline is a powerful grounding crystal that absorbs negative energy. It can be used to absorb electromagnetic radiation from electronic devices. Place a piece of Black Tourmaline near your electronic devices or at the entrance of your home to protect against negative energy.

- Citrine: Citrine is a beautiful yellow crystal that is associated with abundance and prosperity. It promotes success and to attract wealth and abundance. Place a piece of Citrine inside your front door, in your office or near your cash register to promote business success.

- Selenite: Selenite is a high vibrational white crystal that is associated with clarity and purification. Selenite cleanses the energy of a space and promotes mental clarity and focus. Place a piece of Selenite in your home office or study to promote focus and concentration and eradicate any stagnant energy.

- Hematite: Hematite the dark grey or black crystal is associated with grounding and protection.

Clear Quartz

Clear Quartz is a powerful crystal that is known for its ability to amplify and clear energy. Placing Clear Quartz in the corners of a room can help to circulate the energy and create a more balanced and harmonious environment. When energy becomes stagnant in a room, it can create a feeling of heaviness or negativity. By placing Clear Quartz in the corners of the room, you can help to break up this stagnant energy and allow it to flow more freely. Clear Quartz works by absorbing, amplifying, and then releasing energy. When it is placed in the corners of a room, it absorbs the stagnant energy and amplifies it, creating a more powerful force. As the energy is released, it flows more freely throughout the room, creating a more balanced and harmonious environment. In addition to circulating energy, Clear Quartz also helps to clear negative energy from the space. It can absorb negative energy and transform it into positive energy, creating a more positive and uplifting environment. To use Clear Quartz to circulate energy in a room, simply place it in the corners of the room. You can place small Clear Quartz points in each corner or a larger Clear Quartz cluster in a central location. You can also program the Clear Quartz with your intention for the space, such as promoting peace and harmony or attracting abundance. By using Clear Quartz to circulate energy in your home, you can create a more balanced and harmonious environment that promotes emotional and spiritual well-being.

Rose Quartz

Rose Quartz is a beautiful pink crystal that is associated with love, compassion, and emotional healing. Placing Rose Quartz in a child's room can help to promote a loving and nurturing environment, and provide several benefits to the child. Here are some ways that using Rose Quartz in a child's room can help:

- Promotes feelings of love and security: Children need to feel loved and secure in their environment, and Rose Quartz can help to create a sense of warmth and safety. Placing Rose Quartz in the child's room can help to promote feelings of love, trust, and security.

- Encourages emotional healing: Children often experience a range of emotions, and Rose Quartz can help to soothe and heal any emotional wounds. It can help to calm anxiety, ease stress, and promote a sense of peace and tranquillity.

- Improves sleep quality: Children need quality sleep to grow and develop properly, and Rose Quartz can help to promote a restful night's sleep. Its calming energy can help to ease any bedtime fears, nightmares, or anxieties, allowing the child to feel more relaxed and at ease.

- Enhances creativity and imagination: Children have vivid imaginations, and Rose Quartz can help to enhance their creativity and imagination. Its gentle energy can help to inspire the child's creativity, and encourage them to explore their inner world.

To use Rose Quartz in a child's room, you can place it in several different ways. You can place a large Rose Quartz crystal or a Rose Quartz geode on a shelf or table in the room or you can place smaller Rose Quartz stones under the child's pillow or mattress (depending on the age of the child as you do not want the child to swallow the crystal).

What crystal clears negative energy and how to use it and cleans it?

Black Tourmaline is a powerful crystal that is known for its ability to clear negative energy. It can help to transmute negative energy into positive energy, creating a more balanced and harmonious environment. Here's how to use Black Tourmaline to clear negative energy:

- Placement: One way to use Black Tourmaline is to place it in areas where negative energy may be present, such as near electronic devices or in areas of the home where there is a lot of foot traffic. You can also place it at the entrance of your home to help prevent negative energy from entering.

- Meditation: Another way to use Black Tourmaline is to hold it during meditation or place it on the body during energy healing sessions. It can help to absorb negative energy and promote a sense of calm and peace.

- Grids: You can also create a Black Tourmaline grid by placing several Black Tourmaline stones in a specific pattern in a room or around a person's body. This can help to create a strong barrier of protection against negative energy.

To cleanse Black Tourmaline, you can use several methods:

Placing Black Tourmaline outside during a full moon can help to cleanse and recharge the crystal. Simply place it on a windowsill or outside where it can absorb the moonlight.

Smudging: Burning sage or other herbs and passing the Black Tourmaline through the smoke can help to cleanse it of negative energy.

Saltwater: Placing Black Tourmaline in a bowl of saltwater can help to cleanse and recharge the crystal. Be sure to use filtered or distilled water and not tap water, as tap water may contain impurities that can damage the crystal.

In conclusion, Black Tourmaline is a powerful crystal that can help to clear negative energy and promote a sense of calm and peace. It can be used in several different ways, such as placement, meditation, or grids. To cleanse Black Tourmaline, you can use moonlight, smudging, or saltwater.

<u>Cleansing a house of negative energy</u>

Cleansing a house of negative energy can be done using several methods, and it is important to choose a method that resonates with you and your beliefs. Here are some ways to cleanse a house of negative energy:

- Smudging: Smudging is a Native American practice that involves burning herbs, such as Sage, Cedar, or Palo Santo, to purify the air and clear negative energy. To smudge your house, light a bundle of sage or other herb, and then walk around the house, waving the smoke into all corners and areas of the home.

- Salt: Salt is another powerful tool for cleansing negative energy. You can sprinkle salt around the perimeter of your home, and place bowls of salt in each room. After a few hours, you can remove/sweep up the salt and place the discarded salt into the outside rubbish bin away from the house.

- Sound: Sound vibrations can help to clear negative energy from a home. You can use singing bowls, chimes, or even your voice to create sound vibrations in each room of the house.

- Crystals: Certain crystals, such as Black Tourmaline, can help to absorb negative energy. You can place these crystals in different areas of your home or create a crystal grid for the whole house.

- Cleaning: Cleaning your home is another effective way to clear negative energy. Dusting, sweeping, and vacuuming can help to physically remove any negative energy that may be lingering in your home.

- Fresh Air: Opening windows and doors and let fresh air circulate the house to remove stagnant air, place fresh flowers in a vase in your lounge room and a blessing of the house by you.

It is important to keep in mind that cleansing your home of negative energy is an ongoing practice. You can do it regularly or as needed, especially after any stressful or negative events that may have occurred in your home.

In conclusion, there are several ways to cleanse a house of negative energy, including smudging, salt, sound, crystals, and cleaning. Choose a method that resonates with you and your beliefs, and make it a regular practice to help create a peaceful and harmonious environment in your home.

Your Notes:

CHAPTER TWENTY FIVE

Fung Shwa And The Office Environment

Let us now move into a different area, where we can further our expectations into understanding more regarding the unconscious/higher mind and how Fung Shwa improves and adds value to self. You cannot Fung Shwa an office in the same way as a house, as the energy in an office works in the opposite direction. In an office, you are receiving a payment through the investment that you believe yourself to be. You collect those people who can become an asset to you and also to the business. That is why it is called a "business"; whereas, in a home, you are relying on yourself to create your solitude from others in order to release your inner peace.

When I am designing the interior of a business office, I have a selection of plants that I use to help those concerned advance their inner mathematics, through the concentration process that helps them keep their mind alerted to the job at hand. We find that, through the Laws of the Universe, those plants are mathematically applicable to the responsibility that comes with the position at hand. Their mathematical essence becomes a commitment to the office; this helps us house a business that yearns to reach its own attainment, and this is the business that will become a success. If the staff are happy in their positions of employment, the whole business will collect its rewards. I have a series of plants that I use throughout the office; I select the plants depending upon the positions, the workload, and the company's expectation of its workers.

Here is a list of some of the plants that I use depending, on the size of the room and the tasks of those who occupy it during the workday.

Sansevieria (commonly known as the "mother–in-law's tongue") likes to stand behind the others. Any of the Dracaena family – Marginata, Deremensis, and Fragrans, to name just a few – all are used in the Asian influence as plants that attract the vibration of money. My personal favourites are the flax plants and the Cordylines, which alert the unconscious as to what can be achieved by being in their presence (remember the Cordylines at my front door!). Much more advancement exists in this area today, as you have a much broader range of colours to choose from. Also, the definition gives the consumer many more choice as to leaf texture and quality – shiny, matt, stripes, spots, etc.

To complement a reception area, I use two plants only, sometimes one of the above and maybe a spider plant. Why two plants? The number two, through the unconscious/higher mind, is alerting the customer to the relationship which one can achieve with this business. Don't frighten customers away before you begin! Some companies have a lot of plants in the foyer, which can confuse the client entering the building. This energy changes the perspective of the customer's mind as they walk up to the reception area. The number two represents equality, so the new client or customer will feel at ease before any transaction begins. He feels that he will be listened to and heard, not forced into an agreement. Remember, it's the little things that require attention in order to make your business a success! The majority of indoor plants came from the rain forest thousands of years ago; but, in their original environment, they formed their own tribal law. This law has not changed; these plants evolved to complement another species that required a firmament to strengthen its self as well as other species. So it is with the human brain; when many people work in the same energy, we require and request support from each other.

Recently, I received a commission to Fung Shwa a number of office rooms in a large company in Europe. This Company had eighty-four offices distributed in many different areas, and it held the responsibility to look after all of them. You can imagine how many staff they employed, to keep the accounts up to date!

I looked forward to this commission, which gave me the opportunity to explain my repertoire to the company's management, showing them how the energy of Fung Shwa connects to all and what changes they could expect to notice from the outcome of my work. I asked them to wait for thirty to ninety days before they would see the results; finally, they accepted this, and I could begin my work. We began at six in the morning in one of the typing pools of the auditing department, where seventeen people all worked together in the same large room; each member of the pool had a position to fulfil, and then his/her work was passed on to the next desk, etc. – in this way, they were all responsible for their commitment to the auditing department. I asked the manager to explain some of the personalities of these workers; I was interested in who was the talker, who sat back, who used others for their own excuses – the normal office pool "stuff"! I was shown each desk, complete with an explanation of which person worked in each section.

This large room was full of 2–3-metre-high shrubs or small trees clustered around the desks, and many pots with small, spindly plants – some with odd, dead flowers collapsing around the greenery. These pots were placed randomly, filling up most of the room. It looked more like a nursery that had released itself back to the jungle, rather than an auditing room in an office building. With the help of a couple of the workers and a few hefty men, we removed all the foliage from the room and placed it out in the corridor. I then had an opportunity to value the layout of the whole room while it was bare. Just creating this movement certainly changed the energy of the room. I heard a long drawn-out sigh of relief coming from the room. It was right on eight o'clock when the carrier truck came in and removed all the excess plants in the corridor, and, as the last of the old plants plant went out the door, two different men stood there, saying that they had a delivery of new plants and asking where could they put them. They began to wheel in the new plants on large trolleys; these plants all glistened with health and were the most amazing colours, looking vibrant in their brand-new pots. Ranging in height from 50–60 centimetres to 1.5 meters, they were just what I'd ordered. I have yet to meet a country that can match the disciplined mind of Germany; it is so well organized in everything the people accomplish and create. The old plants would be distributed to nursing homes, hospitals, clubs, schools, etc., so they would be of use.

Next, the manager gave me a chart explaining the workflow;

it showed where each person began his/her work, how it moved through each member, and its final outcome. I always start on the left-hand side of the room, as there must be a beginning point in order for the energy to move forward. It is on the left-hand side of the room that our ego looks for its safety zones of comfort. Comfort must be replaced with courage! Thus, we began by moving each desk into a format as to who was responsible for each section; from there, it passed on to the next one, and so on – in this manner, we moved around the room, from desk to desk, until we finished the auditing process.

Then we came to the task of moving all the computers to the appropriate desks. The hours rolled by; slowly, we began to form a circle of energy, where we could see how it completed itself! I asked the woman who was in charge of this department to stand off to the right-hand side of the room, where she could assess the completed work and file all the paperwork to finish the job, as would happen at the end of an actual workday. This large room had a huge responsibility to fulfil within the company, and the staff members who worked in that room were many months behind in their work schedules, as there was so much paperwork to finalize on behalf of everyone that depended on this auditing department. The main reason why I had received the commission to do this job was that they could not find an outlet to advance this group of workers.

This huge room had a small section where the staff could have a coffee break. I moved this section over towards the centre of the right-hand side of the room, where I placed a couple of small round tables and a total of seven chairs. Again, the unconscious/higher mind was at work. They had a coffee machine on hand and available for use throughout the day. I placed the clock at eye level on the wall opposite the entrance into this section, which would consciously remind the staff of the time every time they entered the area; this would help them realize that they were entering a place of respite for the moment. One selection of plants was brought into this area, and, again, it was a group of three. Why? The number three (3), when decoded through the language of the unconscious/higher mind, represents the Collective Mind, and so it autonomically keeps the mind prepared to connect to each moment.

I wanted to anoint the staff, through the respite that the employees earn when they are in their break room. (More detailed explanations on numbers appear in my book "Decoding Sacred Alphabet and Numerology".) The only difference was that I introduced another plant into this area, which I did in order to break up the conformity of energy so that the unconscious/higher mind could take notice of the change in the plan. Usually, I placed one of the Aralia species amongst the Cordylines or Dracaenas. This had to be smaller than the other two. Why? Aralias have leaves of seven finger points; these are flat, wide, broad leaves that would allow the mind to relax just for a brief moment. These plants look like open hands with the fingers outstretched. I refer to the Aralia as my "pause plant". The numbers have to be in sequence to the people who enter the room, in order for them to hold their selves into an abeyance of each moment. For this same reason, these same plants are also excellent for the lounge room and bedroom.

Finally, after many hours of exertion, we could see how each entry of work entered the room and was completed, so that the final account of the work could move on and out to the next appropriate section of the company. I had to explain this, every step of the way, to the people who were there to assist me; they found it fascinating to discover that, as the energy came into the room and circulated, it also had to have the freedom to leave. I now had the chance to move in the appropriate plants; we grouped all of them in threes, setting them in certain sections of the room and placing them near those workers who were on my list. These were the workers who sat back and relied on others to carry them; I chose to place smaller plants to surround them. They had to be motivated into accomplishing through their own responsibility; placing these smaller plants nearby gave their ego a shot of compulsive behaviour to try to strive a little bit harder. They wanted to feel as good as the others. Those who tried to control others, and could not focus on their own workload, had no plants around them at all. They were naked. And the rest of the plants were distributed accordingly in order to balance the room. It all sounds terrible, doesn't it? Just by using a selection of the plant species that create a relationship to balance the mind, we could change the communal thinking.

As the workers filed out of the room after completing their day, I grouped a variety of plants to the left of the door that was different from what they had in the rest of the room, so that their conscious mind – or ego – could view them as they walked out the door. Why? I had to unconsciously change their attitude, as they had finished the work for what they were employed to do; therefore, their mind could swing back into where it found a comfort zone, and they could reconnect back into their own personalities of self!

I narrowed the plants down to seven areas, which were spread throughout the room. Why seven? The unconscious/higher mind lives in numbers, and the number seven (7) is a reflection of energy that relates to the seven seals or chakras. The number seven (7) also relates to the inner teacher, and, when we are working in group energy, the ego of each is out to impress others, and this creates competition. One is on one's best behaviour when there is a challenge to urge, or surge, us forward. This is the "Holy Grail" at work.

And, so after many strenuous hours, the job was completed, and the workers and I went out to a restaurant for a nourishing meal. I explained the methods of my work, including how the energy is conduited (by means of its own expression) around the room to affect every person in the room. This telepathic resonance communicates and collects through the unconscious/higher mind, which will become the new value of the room. There were many sniggers of disbelief that evening, but this has happened most of my life – and it will not ease until each person can begin to see and believe in their own results.

Exactly three weeks to the day, I received a phone call from the company manager, asking me for an appointment so that he could discuss some things with me. I knew that if I made a success of this job, other jobs would follow. The manager came to see me at the appointed time, I invited him in and offered him coffee. He sipped his coffee, sitting quietly and just looking at me. As I waited for his conversation to open up, he smiled at me and said, "I cannot believe it! I cannot believe it!" he said to me. "Do you know that we have caught up with months of back work, and all in three short weeks? And today, a couple of the workers came to me so excited about the achievements that they have been able to accomplish, asking me if they could stay back a couple of hours a week to see the rest of the bookwork completed. Do you know, Omni, that they are actually smiling as they are working? And another thing – people are coming from all over the building and looking to see what all the fuss is all about. Even the CEO paid us a visit! I have tried to explain this 'phenomena' to him, but I am so illiterate as to this information. And you asked for ninety days to see the benefits!"

After that, the next room was placed before me; again, it was a huge success for all concerned. The staff came to see me, and I received many accolades and gifts of flowers from them, also over the next few weeks, as to how they had changed their minds regarding not only their workload, also their personal life as well.

Your Notes:

CHAPTER TWENTY SIX

Colour For The Office

When we come to the colour of the office walls, we should learn to use the subtle lemon tones in the secretary's office; as this colour activates the mind. If the office has group energy, then again, I suggest the lighter lemon toning, as this keeps the staff occupied and focused on their own workload. It activates the mind, but it will not interfere with other workers.

If we put beige, white, or cream walls in the office, the staff will be too busy creating difficulties around focusing on the work at hand. We can also work with timber, using a harmonizing colour in the CEO's office, to contribute to the work of the day.

I did a feasibility study for a group in Japan in the early '90s, after suggesting to the management that they paint the walls of their offices a flat pale lemon with gloss white door trims. The difference was huge: After 90 days, the workload had upgraded itself by more than 30 percent. The lemon colour stimulated the ego and urged the workers forward; the white gloss around the doors reflected back into the room to keep the higher mind permanently open and focused on the job at hand. We are learning to understand the Collective Inheritance of the unconscious/higher mind as we evolve – that is, as to how it holds every memory that is mathematically created on the planet. Colours play an important role in keeping it focused on the energy at hand. Yellow is the colour that stimulates the education system of one's life. Through my own personal experiences working with children who have difficulties with their learning process – and, thus, have a tendency to walk away from disciplining themselves – I place an A4-size piece of lemon-coloured paper in front of them so that they can focus on the colour. Of course, they turn away from the colour at first; but, with perseverance, I train them to look at the paper. This makes them squeamish at first, but, once we overcome this hurdle, they are able, in time, to become stimulated to release the excuses and pressure that they have placed around the hypothalamus gland – and once they do that, they are able to re-educate themselves.

The CEO's office (or the office of whoever is the "boss") should always be painted in white, with subtle grey toning, as these two colours relate to the essence of that person – his/her "formula", one could say – and they also represent their balanced mind. This individual is there to promote his/her ideas back to the staff. Grey is the main colour of the imperial essence, and this colour is the impression of what we have achieved, which we then release out to others. It can be highlighted with black, white, gold, or silver – all these colours complement and enhance our imperial behaviour.

In Europe, they create their offices with mellow timber, usually from the oak, beech, or maple trees; this is the boss's tree of knowledge, and he/she can gain silence and perspective through the genre framed around him/her.

It is interesting to realize that the unconscious/higher mind is in a perfect relationship to the energy that we refer to as our Soul, and this is always working for us. It is in the wings waiting for us to be still or silent, in order to allow the electrical conduit system to start triggering a response within us, which the majority of you only become aware of when you are asleep.

Fung Shwa is a biological plan of human thinking that brings all our wisdom up into the royal behaviour of self. When we make ourselves aware of it, yet refuse to listen to the positive ideas that are presented to us, we automatically degrade ourselves, and then we slip back 10 degrees – means that there is no change in our lives; we stay on the same tepid level. What is even more interesting is how the unconscious/higher mind tries to show us what colours we need to wrap around us, in order to open our mind up into its next equation. Those who don't want to accept their daily life instil; the fears of the past generations that are still harboured within them. There must be a reason to the season of each thought, in its moment.

When we come up against a colour that seems abrasive to the mind, what mindset are we in that is not open to collect and release our next thought? Every thought requires our attention, in order for us to move forward. These colours are situated in the body through the arching of our covenant, which is exactly the same as a rainbow forming in the sky.

We begin with the colour red, which is situated between the upper inner thighs, and then we move into the colour orange, which is created through the surging of our sexual feelings provided to the mind. The next colour is yellow, which stimulates our inner education system. The next is emerald-green; again, our feelings step forward as we learn to accept and open up our heart. From here, we move up into the throat area, which creates the colour blue. We begin to speak our wisdom, and now you know why the colours of King Tut's mask are in the royal colours of speaking through the higher mind or Soul energy. Lilac is the last colour we ignite, and it is where we have a permanent geomancy in connection to our thoughts; this is always on standby, waiting to point us in the right direction.

Your Notes:

CHAPTER TWENTY SEVEN

Fung Shwa—A Small Clothing Retail Store

The energy of Fung Shwa can help create a harmonious and prosperous environment for a small retail store that sells clothing. Following are some guidelines:

- Create a welcoming entrance: The entrance of a store is where the energy enters, and it should be inviting and attractive. Hang a wind chime or a bell at the entrance to draw positive energy into the store. If your store is inside a shopping centre, place a plant near the entrance to bring in fresh energy.

- Signage of the store name should be easy to read and directly over the front door or close to one side. Walls should be coloured in white or soft lemon to stimulate the mind into focusing on what they are looking for.

- The flow of energy in the store should be optimized to ensure a smooth shopping experience. Make sure that the aisles are clear and uncluttered to allow the energy to flow freely. Avoid placing any obstacles in the way of the entrance or exit of the store.

- Draw customers in by creating a primary focal point with an interesting display.

- Display clothing attractively: The clothing in the store should be displayed attractively to draw the customers in. Use lighting to highlight the clothing and create a warm and welcoming ambiance. If your back door is in direct alignment with your front door, arrange displays in angles, or circular motion in order to correct the energy exiting directly from front to back of the store.

- Regularly change window displays.

- Another important factor to consider is the lighting in the store. Adequate lighting can enhance the energy flow and create a welcoming atmosphere. It is recommended to use soft, natural lighting rather than harsh fluorescent lights, as they can create an uncomfortable and sterile feeling.

- The placement of mirrors can also be important in a clothing retail store. Mirrors can be used strategically to reflect light and create the illusion of a larger space. They can also be placed in locations where customers can see themselves trying on the clothes, which can boost their confidence and ultimately lead to a purchase.

- Keep the space clutter-free and maintain a balanced energy flow. Avoid overloading display racks with too many clothes or creating cramped spaces for customers to navigate. Creating open spaces and allowing for natural flow can enhance the energy of the space and create a positive shopping experience for customers.

- Cash Register: Position the cash register in a location that allows the store owner to see the entrance and exit of the store. This will give a sense of security and control to the store owner.

- Have friendly staff. Customers feel appreciated when acknowledged with a smile. An atmosphere that is welcoming helps bring in more customers. A greeting when the customer walks in and a "thank you" when the customer leaves.

Displaying clothes

In a clothing retail store, displaying clothes in a way that is aesthetically pleasing and easy for customers to navigate is important for creating a harmonious shopping environment. The placement and arrangement of clothing can also affect the flow of energy in the space.

To start, it is recommended to display clothes in colour-coded sections or by type (i.e. shirts, pants, dresses) to create a visually appealing and organized display. The colour scheme used in the display should also be in harmony with the energy of the store, as well as the intended purpose of the clothes being sold.

Change your clothing display, rotating the merchandise is one way to keep fresh energy circulating and stimulates sales.

Design several pathways within the store to make it interesting (not one straight line).

By following these guidelines, a small retail store that sells clothes can create a harmonious and prosperous environment for both the customers and the store owner.

Your Notes:

CHAPTER TWENTY EIGHT

Fung Shwa—A Small Retail Store That Sells Shoes

When it comes to a small retail store that sell shoes, the store can benefit from the proper arrangement and placement of the items in the store. Here are some guidelines:

- Declutter and organize: Keep the store organized and free of clutter. This allows the energy to flow smoothly and freely throughout the space.

- Lighting: Make sure the store is well-lit. Bright and inviting lighting can attract customers, and can also enhance the overall energy of the store. Wall display is usually covered with a storehouse of many shoes ceiling to floor and is not even seen by the customer unless there is good lighting.

- Display: Display the shoes in an aesthetically pleasing manner. Arrange them in a way that catches the customer's attention and makes it easy for them to find what they are looking for.

- Cash register: Position the cash register in a location that allows the store owner to see the entrance and exit of the store. This will give a sense of security and control to the store owner.

- Mirrors: Place mirrors in strategic locations to reflect the shoes and create the illusion of a larger space.

- Plants: Introduce some greenery into the store with plants. Make up a small display on a table of a plant around three-quarters of a meter high, with a few smart exclusive shoes in attendance (placement), matching and complimenting both men and women, and then watch how many people stop and take notice of what you have accomplished. This can create a sense of freshness and promote healthy energy flow.

Shoe Display

When it comes to displaying shoes in a small retail store, the way they are arranged can make a big difference in attracting customers and increasing sales. Display the shoes in an aesthetically pleasing manner. Arrange them in a way that catches the customer's attention and makes it easy for them to find what they are looking for.

One effective technique is to arrange the shoes in a way that tells a story or evokes a certain feeling, such as pairing summer sandals with beach decor or arranging hiking boots with outdoor-themed elements. Another way to create a visually appealing display is to use props such as risers or mannequin legs to showcase the shoes at different heights and angles. It is also important to ensure that the shoes are organized by style and size, with clear signage to help customers find what they need quickly and easily. By taking the time to arrange shoes in an attractive and organized manner, retailers can enhance the shopping experience for their customers and increase their chances of making a sale.

CHAPTER TWENTY NINE

Fung Shwa—A Small Cafe

Fung Shwa can be applied to create a welcoming and harmonious environment in a café. One of the most important aspects is the layout of the space, which should encourage the flow of positive energy, or Chi.

The entrance of the café should be well-lit and unobstructed, with a clear path leading into the main seating area. The seating area should be arranged in a way that allows for comfortable movement and social interaction. Round or oval tables are considered preferable to square or rectangular ones, as they promote a sense of unity and inclusivity. In terms of decor, natural materials are encouraged. Wooden tables and chairs, potted plants, and water features can all help to create a calming and inviting atmosphere. Artwork and signage should be tasteful and not overwhelming, with a focus on positive messaging.

The location of the café's kitchen and restroom facilities should also be considered. The kitchen should ideally be located towards the back of the café, to avoid disruptions to the flow of energy. Restrooms should be clean, well-lit, and located away from the seating area.

Finally, attention should be paid to the café's lighting and music. Lighting should be warm and inviting, without being too dim or too bright. Music should be calming and unobtrusive, and kept at a reasonable volume to allow for conversation.

By applying these guidelines, a café can create a space that not only looks appealing but also promotes a sense of balance, harmony, and positive energy flow.

<u>What colours should be used in the café?</u>

The colours in a café can have a significant impact on the energy and atmosphere of the space. Warm and welcoming colours such as yellow, orange, and red can stimulate the appetite and create a lively atmosphere, while cooler colours like blue and green can promote relaxation and calmness. Earth tones like brown and beige can also create a warm and inviting environment. When choosing colours, it's important to consider the overall theme and mood of the café, as well as the type of customers you want to attract.

Your Notes:

CHAPTER THIRTY

How many of you walk into a room and say "good morning" or "good night" to a room/house/office?

How many of you walk into a room and say "good morning" or "good night" to a room/house/office? A room you have created/work is a parallel world of yours. This volume of energy is yours! Does it really work on your behalf?

I explain this in my business seminars when I teach people how to walk into their office for the first time. This is something they – and you – should do each day! Have you placed your intention into that room, where you will spend the next eight hours of your day (or night, in the case of your bedroom)? By doing this, you enhance your energy, as well as the energy of the room, and you bring them into an agreement with one another. It does not matter how many people work in that same area, if it is an office. By acknowledging your area, the room begins to look for you in the morning, and you will find that your day is no longer a burden to you as it was before.

Focus your intention on yourself, and you become the winner! Sounds ridiculous, doesn't it? Please trust me, and you will be amazed at my words! Thousands of my students are already doing this all around the world, and there is no way that they would go back to their old ways! Promotions have come to them from all angles. In time you, will walk into the room and just nod to it; that is all! The mathematics has taken over, and it is working on your behalf!

<u>Focus your intention on yourself is a powerful practice</u>

Focusing your intention on yourself is a powerful practice that allows you to prioritize your needs, desires, and personal growth. By directing your attention inward, you create space for self-reflection, self-care, and self-improvement. It involves tuning out external distractions and turning your focus towards your thoughts, emotions, and aspirations. When you focus your intention on yourself, you become more aware of your values, strengths, and areas for development. This heightened self-awareness enables you to make conscious choices aligned with your authentic self and create a fulfilling life. It empowers you to set meaningful goals, cultivate positive habits, and pursue your passions with greater clarity and purpose. Taking time to focus on yourself also promotes mental, emotional, and spiritual well-being, allowing you to nurture a deeper connection with yourself and live a more intentional and fulfilling life.

Placing your intention into the room you are going to work in can greatly influence the energy and outcomes of your day. Here are some steps to help you do so:

- Set your intention: Before entering the room, take a moment to clarify your intention for the day. What positive results do you want to achieve? Whether it's increased productivity, creativity, or a positive work environment, clearly state your intention in your mind.

- Create a positive environment: As you enter the room, take a few deep breaths to centre yourself. Remove any clutter or distractions that may hinder your focus. Arrange the space in a way that promotes productivity and supports your work goals.

- Visualize success: Close your eyes for a moment and visualize yourself accomplishing your tasks with ease and efficiency. Imagine the room filled with positive energy and see yourself thriving in this environment. Visualizing success helps align your subconscious mind with your intention.

- Use affirmations: Repeat positive affirmations related to your intention. For example, you can say statements like "I am focused and productive" or "I attract positive outcomes in my work." Affirmations help reinforce your intention and create a positive mindset.

- Take breaks for realignment: Throughout the day, take short breaks to realign your intention. Step away from your work area, take a few deep breaths, and remind yourself of your purpose and goals. This helps maintain your focus and ensures you stay on track.

- Remember, placing your intention into the room is a personal practice, and you can adapt it to suit your preferences and beliefs. The key is to be present, focused, and intentional about the energy you bring into the space.

Your Notes:

CHAPTER THIRTY ONE

Fung Shwa and Money

By incorporating Fung Shwa, one can attract abundance and prosperity into their life, including money.

One of the simplest ways to attract money is to clear clutter from your home, particularly in the wealth area. The wealth area is located in the far left corner of your space as you stand at the entrance facing inward. Keep this area clean, organized, and free of any clutter. Additionally, incorporate the colour green into this space, as it symbolizes wealth and abundance. You can do this by adding green plants or using green accents in the decor.

Another way to attract money is to use the power of the five elements of Feng Shui. In the wealth area, use the wood element, which symbolizes growth and vitality. You can add wood elements by incorporating plants, wooden furniture, or even a wooden sculpture. Water is another powerful element in Feng Shui, and it represents abundance and prosperity. Placing a small water fountain in the wealth area can help attract money and create a flow of positive energy. You can also incorporate the water element through the use of mirrors or glass decor. Make sure that the entrance to your home is welcoming and unobstructed. A clear and open entrance allows for positive energy to flow into your space, including the energy of abundance and prosperity.

<u>The Metaphysics Of Money And Thought</u>

Excerpt from the book: "Decoding Thought", Chapter 14. The Metaphysics Of Money And Thought, O.M. Kelly.

Understanding the metaphysics of money and thought is essential to achieving financial abundance and success. Our thoughts and beliefs about money can have a profound impact on our financial situation. By understanding the underlying metaphysical principles that govern money, we can gain greater clarity in our relationship with money, and the role it plays in our lives. Money is not just a physical object or a means of exchange; it is an energy that is influenced by our thoughts and beliefs. By changing our mindset towards money, we can attract more abundance and prosperity into our lives.

The metaphysical principles of manifestation and abundance show us that we have the power to create the financial reality that we desire. By harnessing the power of our thoughts and beliefs, we can manifest wealth and abundance into our lives, and overcome any financial obstacles that may arise. Understanding the metaphysics of money and thought is a crucial step in achieving financial success and living a life of abundance.

I write a different version to what you have probably read before regarding money. Again, I speak through the Laws of the Universe as to how we learn to understand this energy that comes only from the left hemisphere of the brain.

Following are questions and answers with information on the power of this energy which we refer to as money and how we can attract it to our self. This chapter is brief and very direct for the person who has difficulties with respecting the money they earn.

Most people who inherit their money from their past generations very quickly consume it. Why? They have never had to earn it. So, how do they know how to respect it? To become a winner of this energy is to serve oneself, but to become a servant to others means that we have upheld our own consequences and freely gifted away what was rightfully ours.

To serve ourselves we have to delve deep into the abyss of self. This gives us the priority right to act on our own behalf and our Individual Universal Law and the Laws of the universe.

My Grandmother's advice:

Aim for the highest
There's room at the top.

My Grandmother wrote those words in my autograph book on my ninth birthday and it took me forty years to understand what she had written to me. I knew that verse by heart throughout my childhood and so I always reached up; I did not know what I was reaching for, but I reached anyway. Those words finally measured in me an unfolding of my own intelligence, through the discovery of me walking up into my own unconscious/higher mind through the education and finally the evolution of believing in self.

Let's talk about money. You are your own bank and your thinking controls that bank. Give to yourself in a loving and respectful way and money will come back to you tenfold. Believe in yourself and understand how that respect for money works for you. When decoded through the Sacred Alphabet the word "Money" represents: Through Mastering the Oracle I Nourish and Energize my Yearning. Let me explain. When we learn something and understand what we have learned, we cannot forget it. Once we have understood, it becomes complete and then we have the pleasure of acting it. That process may take years or moments; the choice is entirely yours. The moment that you hesitate through yearning about how to understand your subject, the energy then falters and you have to repeat the lesson over again.

During our early years of education, our teachers were constantly assessing us by exams in order for us to understand and know that particular subject. Over time, we set ourselves a standard of knowledge and wisdom regarding the subjects that we want to take responsibility for. Your whole life has been filled with many experiences of learning, so, it is with learning about our self!

I am a trained and educated Metaphysician, so I will speak to you through my own intelligence in the way that I was educated. It was an extremely long and difficult Academic Universal Education of Mathematics, the Sciences and Physics, as I was introduced into the next evolution of how we understand our Soul.

The Soul is the reason we are all here on this planet and if we don't have one then we are not here, we are dead!

It is as simple as that. Our Soul is our life force; it is what keeps us in an upright majestic position with our feet firmly on the ground. That energy has electromagnetic fields of force and those forces are the repetitious performance of our past generations. Every memory of humanities earnings is embedded in the nuclei of each cell in our body! This is known as our Divine Energy. It is our journey to walk through our life to desire to define the divine. There is a season for every reason that we can think of and there is an answer to every question that we ask.

My education took nine years of my life to study and to then be approved and accepted by my teachers in order for me to become a Teacher of the Collective Consciousness. There is only about 1% of humanity that understands this collective inheritance, so I have had a huge responsibility to release this information to you. I cannot sit back on my laurels through 99% of humanity still not understanding why they are here or what purpose they must live through, in order for this planet to evolve!

Everything on the earth is coded through the mathematics, which collects itself through the consciousness. In the world of mathematics there is no emotion attached or ego to interfere with, so it always remains our pure truth. It is above the use of our everyday wisdom, so we have to earn our responsibilities of how we collect our thoughts which create our sentences, in order for us to get where we want to be.

I had previously thought that because I was on my quest, I had to be poor and become a servant to others, but I know now that this type of thinking is not quite correct. Our physical world does not stand still when we contact our inner pathway, it keeps right on moving and we must move along with it. We cannot stop or interfere with that Law of the Universe; we can learn to understand and accept it. If you think poor then you attract poverty. If you sacrifice to yourself then you are a fool and a fool and his money are soon parted.

A sacrifice is the depletion of self, a lowering of self, where you live your life as a servant to others. I made a sacrifice of myself through my poverty thinking, so my program had to be totally reversed; I had to grow up and learn the respect for self. I found a new growth of salutations (respect for myself) that I could adhere to and live up to that balanced and harmonized thinking. When I realized that I did not have to live my life thinking with a pauper like attitude, my life changed dramatically.

Now that I understand the energy of money, it flows to me and that money gives me freedom of choice, freedom to act and freedom to be. When money comes to you, thank yourself for what you have attracted to yourself, as it is an answer that salutes your questions. That answer is an ending and from endings, new beginnings are waiting to occur. When I fall out of balance with myself, the flow of money stops automatically; that is the Law of the Universe returning my thoughts to me. I had to learn to allow my urges their freedom and rewards.

Money is manifested through your thinking; it is a thought force that releases your energy. You create disease in your body through your thinking, and in the same way you also create money or a lack of it. Some people state: "Oh God, I will never have any money," and with that kind of thinking, they never will.

When you are on your life's quest, you learn to accept, through your new responsibility, that all these energies through your thinking are your own; they are the reflections of your thinking. They are the karma that you innocently give to yourself. If you think fearfully about money, then money will think fearfully about you. Your fear regarding money is an energy force of you not believing in self, so money will not come to you if you are too afraid to accept it. Hide from money and it will hide from you.

Through your belief in self, and through your accepting your intellectual advantages for your own personal gain, you will attract the gifts of the universe that have been stored for you. Your money, or lack of it, reflects your belief in self. Money is a law unto itself, and if you understand that law, then money is free to come to you. Learn to play the game.

In summary money is earned through your thinking, planning,

creating and becoming. The money that comes to you is in accordance with the level of your intelligence that you have allowed for yourself. Money is an energy force that works with us; it is a living matter. It is free energy and that energy is given to us freely if we work within our own boundaries. It is when we step outside our self that the laws of karma automatically adjust our flow.

The Universal Bank

One of my first lessons about money came in the week before I left Australia for Europe. A beautiful young woman came up and said to me, "What is the worry that I sense around you?" I replied, "I am going to Europe next week to give a series of lectures, and I have a fear about not having enough money to live on while I am there." The woman said, "Do you know that there is a universal bank available to every human and it is open twenty-four hours a day? My mother taught me that when I was leaving my own village in Morocco to venture out into the world."

The thought of a universal bank had never entered my head, so I asked her how much money that bank had. She told me that it held enough for every human on the planet to each have three million dollars in their back pocket. That was the most important lesson of my life regarding money, so where the hell was my share? And more importantly who had it all?

I had struggled financially for over forty years and I now know why. It was because I was not ready to accept the responsibility that placed me, in front of the universal bank. I had not earned my interest and so the bank could not pay me for what I had not earned. That interest only arrived through the acceptance of understanding myself. As I cleared one dilemma, another one started as I was busily manifesting it to be that way. It took time for me to see what I was busily preparing for me to inherit, and then to find the courage to walk away from my old ways of thinking. The more occupied my mind focused on the attention before me; the busier I became and I found at the end of the week that the money had measured itself according to my thoughts. It was such a nice surprise to see the result.

I now know from experience that the universal bank doors really are open twenty-four hours a day. My name is in the record books of that bank and the more powerful I become in my thinking, the more powerful my name is pronounced in those records, the more I must receive. I know that this money in the universal bank is for me, as it is a part of the three million dollars that I am entitled to. I saw your name alongside mine in those records too. Look at the codes for three million dollars. There is 3+000,000 which adds up to six (6) zeros. Through the codes of Sacred Numerology, the number three (3) is my collective mind and the six (6) zeros represent to me that I am mastering the energy that is instilled in my soul. That is quite an achievement to live up to.

When we have accepted the responsibility of self, we earn the respect of money and it slides towards us. I have learned that if I want money, I accrue the value of what I am asking for. My energy has to be focused when I ask for money; it has to be balanced in order for me to claim that reflection of my inner self. With a balanced mind you are, and as you think, so too you create and as you ask, so too you receive.

You are relying on yourself to open the door of your mind. Do not allow money to control you, you must learn to be in control of your money. Learn to bank on yourself, as your greatest natural resource, is you! We have the opportunity to create in the moment and understand that you can have, do and think how you want things to be, to create your own lifestyle or business. It is only through the acceptance and belief of self, that our earnings become greater.

Debts that you have already created are yesterday's thinking. Yesterday is over, so your responsibility must now live up to those debts and you must follow through. Keep your mind in the moment as this moment is the doorway to your future. Give credit to yourself and watch how your money grows. My grandmother taught me as a child to pick up my pennies as my pounds have the strength to look after themselves.

Questions and Answers:

Here are some examples of questions that I have been asked

regarding money and I hope that the answers will answer some of your questions.

Question: Money is very important to me, but sometimes I worry that there will not be enough of it to sustain the lifestyle that I currently have. Is that wrong?

Answer: If you are afraid of becoming nothing, then nothing will come to you. Rephrase your thought and say to yourself without any fear, "I like the way I live, so I will live the way I like." Through that statement, you perform one of the most powerful rituals on the planet where you are connecting to your inner Oracle. You have spoken your question and given yourself the answer, so you have balanced your power and attracted the Oracle, which in turn releases itself to you. If you are in your truth, then you are free to attract your inheritance. Trust yourself to attract money and stop feeling unworthy of it.

Question: I worry that I will be judged because I have too much money.

Answer: When you know that you are worthy, the Law of the Universe returns to who you are and how you think. Do not be concerned about what others think of your money as you have a priority right to inherit and collect your own earnings.

Question: Why is it that sometimes when I ask the universe for something, I don't get it?

Answer: That is because you have not asked in the correct way. There is some part of you that is out of balance, so retrace your thoughts and harmonize your fear and emotions. When you ask where you went wrong, return your thoughts back into yourself. It is your fear and not your emotions that pull you down, as your fear suppresses your emotions. Those feelings of unworthiness that you have are your belief that you are not good enough; you will find that those beliefs stop everything from happening for you. You are bringing your old fears in and saying, "I am not good enough, I am waiting for something to happen to me." Reframe your thinking to positive self-talk and believe in self.

Question: I know that I am as I am, seeking myself and that I must have an interior balance. I also know that in my creation of that balance I make good and bad things happen, but who makes the rules about what is good and what is bad?

Answer: Your judgment of others creates the good and the bad. God or the Collective Consciousness creates the Laws of the Universe, but only you have the right to make your own law in regards to what is good and right for yourself (your Individual Universal Law). We cannot say that one person is better than another, as that is out of our jurisdiction. If someone else seems better than you, it is only because they have balanced their thinking more than you have. You have given them the priority right to do so, through your fear of self, to stand up and become superior to you.

Question: Is it okay to play the Stock Market in order to get money?

Answer: Everything is okay. Are you okay regarding your investment? Are you prepared to win or lose? Where is your thinking on this? It is a feeling of self-worth that attracts us to the stock markets.

Let me explain that through a story: I counselled three members of the same family who had lost one million dollars of an inheritance on the stock market. It was given as an educational allowance in trust for their children, from their parents. They came to me and said, "We put the money on the stock market and have lost everything in three months! Can you help us to get it back please?" I said to them, "You deserved to lose it! That money was a gift and a gift is something that you had received for your next generation. It was not given to you; it was not yours to do as you like, your parents made a decision to leave that money in your care for the children's safe keeping. You reached beyond your own Oracle, your own expectations, and that money was not for you to squander or pander to." Believe it or not, I have heard exactly this same story a thousand times.

You weren't ready for that inheritance. You had not evolved enough into the hierarchal mind of self, to the level of the inheritance that you were given. You entrusted somebody else to look after your money; you sold yourself short! Somebody had to benefit from that inheritance, but it wasn't you. It was a great inheritance to the company who wanted the money, as that company's collective consciousness was much higher than those who had inherited the money.

There can only be one winner in a partnership, but as colleagues we all have the same chance to benefit. Why? We have introduced the word respect in order to become united with one another, where all of us in the same company are equal and that is the aim of the Universal Law. We pay much more attention when it is our own savings that we are dealing with, as those savings are a result of our own self - worth!

Most people lose an inheritance as they do not understand the cause and effect of the Law of the Universe. Look at the stock market today and see the results where millions of people have lost billions of dollars. I have people coming to me all of the time who have lost their life savings, inheritance, or some large amount of money on the stock market. That is because they were living in their own fear and could not fully trust the energy of their money working on its own behalf. They don't come to me when they are making their money; I am of no interest to them then.

There are many winners on the stock market and good luck to them; they were ready for the consequences of their inheritance. Did you know that 99% of people who play the stock market do it to enhance their freedom? They are hoping that their money will work for them.

Those who lost their finances took a gamble; they were innocently searching for a "get rich quick" scheme or that quick turnover where money works for them without them working to earn their money. Many of those people said "I thought I would invest the money for safe keeping." Well, it was safe, but it was safe in someone else's hands. They lost it through their trust in someone else with their money instead of trusting themselves to succeed in their own endeavours. Success cannot happen through that kind of thinking. We tip our own scales through lack of wisdom, not knowledge. Your investment represents your belief in self.

Question: If I inherit money from my family and use it for myself is that okay?

Answer: It is perfect; giving it to yourself is a gift of freedom; it is an atonement of all your personalities (aspects of self) receiving the benefits at the same time. Salute yourself!

Question: How can we avoid falling down the ladder of success?

Answer: Check that your ladder is on stable ground and your foundations are clear and strong. The ladder cannot slip if the belief in self is there to support it. Hear your own voice and judge only yourself.

It is your choice how pleased you are with the amount of money you do or do not have. The moment that you move beyond fear and emotions is when you are stepping up your inner ladder to become equivalent to the same vibration as money, where you and money must become one. Through the Laws of Attraction, you must hold that thought and feel it, become the thought and allow it; only then do you have the right to create it. Money must return to you, if you are of a higher vibration than it is; that is the Law of the Universe.

I can talk about peace, love and light to make you feel good, or I can talk about common sense and you will eventually feel even better. While I was doing the peace, love and light trip, I was flat broke. I screamed to God, "I have studied for over nine years to accept this gift of knowledge in order to teach humanity, when will I receive my emolument?" He replied to me, "When you get out there and work for it, and through your wisdom accruing itself, then you will know you have earned it."

It was then I discovered that money was not going to just fall down from the sky; I had to put my right foot forward to take my next positive step. The moment that I committed to something to benefit myself it happened, the moment that I stopped worrying about money, it presented itself to me.

The moment I realized that every dollar I spent on myself to benefit my own life, it doubled. If I have no fear and do not let suppressed emotions get in the way, then every day becomes my learned success.

It is the childish attitude of your innocence over fear and emotions not balancing, which creates your lack of money. The more you know and understand about yourself, the easier it becomes within; you cannot act before you understand. You have to empower yourself and the only way you can do that is through your expectations of what you would like tomorrow to echo back to you.

Money is not here for just a few; it is here freely to assist those who understand what it is. The energy of money works in collaboration with us when we know who we are. Do not allow your old fear to take over magnificent opportunities that are available to you. "Aim for the highest, there's room at the top" sets an empirical state of mind for you to endow.

Question: How does our consciousness make the previous thought shrink in order to allow the next one to manifest itself?

Answer: Yesterday must give way to today; yesterday's thought is old news and takes its place in your memory banks. When we create something new in our life, we have already experienced, it finds its own hollow and seats itself. If the thoughts were pleasant then we have the opportunity to enhance them; if they were unpleasant then we tend to shy away from them.

Consciousness expands itself moment-by-moment. When

we have completed one thought, the next thought that we have built up through our inner library presents itself to us. Don't hang on to the past as it will hold you back; you cannot remain the same.

The more you respect yourself, the more positive the next thought will be. The more positive and condensed you are in your thinking, the more powerful that thought then becomes and the more it must be returned to you. You are in charge of and responsible for every thought that comes into your mind. Why would you let yourself down by ignoring yourself?

Question: How can I access this fear that I have about not being able to make money?

Answer: Believe in yourself. Fear only comes from the left brain, but you still have a right brain, so activate it into where you have the possibilities to learn about the creation of self.

When we have $20,000 in the bank, we feel quietly comfortable, and when that money grows to $40,000, we feel even more comfortable. After we get to $40,000, we then want $80,000. This then harmonizes our comfort zones and these zones give us a sense of procured (something you have obtained by care or effort) security. This is where our intelligence or light begins to release and you will notice that others are drawn to your attention. They seem to be able to sense, on an unconscious/higher mind level, that you are saluting yourself. You are saluting your own royal behaviour and other people start to be attracted towards your light. The Universe is energy and as our thinking world is within, it also reflects the world without.

Question: I have money problems. Can you help me by looking into my future to see if I have any money coming to me?

Answer: I don't see any money coming, as you have just shown me your future. You have predicted it yourself by saying that you have money problems. By admitting to that statement, you have stepped into your own negativity and stopped the flow of money coming into your life. Why would you want to create that? Respect yourself and accept the changes. Many people have come to me and said that they were told that they would receive an endowment and are still waiting for it to happen! The endowment we receive is regarding your progress and prosperity according to your own intellectual quest. It is natural that the receiver sees only the prosperity regarding financial advancement, not the prosperity of you earning your own state of grace! The moment that you doubt yourself or try to put the responsibility of your lack of money onto someone or something else, you stop the flow coming to you.

When you think a negative thought, change your thinking. When you have balanced your mind, start thinking about what you wish to create for the betterment of yourself and the moment you see that picture, you have begun to visualize your future. Now, bring that vision towards you, don't walk towards it. When you have accepted the responsibility of that vision the money must come to you; this is how the universe works for us. Step-by-step we are given our responsibilities.

Question: I want to believe that money has Karma, so does the way we do things have any effect on the Karma of money?

Answer: Karma is energy attracting attention and everything on this planet is the result of Karma; it is the cause of the affect. You are an equal spark of the Collective Consciousness and the Karma you receive is the result of your consciousness. You are the anti-matter and money is the matter. Matter cannot manifest itself without the anti-matter creating itself! Therefore, the Karma belongs to you and not the money

Whilst you are keeping yourself in the dark, learn to understand what barriers you are restricting yourself with. Do not run from money; it is through you releasing your fear and stepping up into your light that money has the possibility of presenting itself to you. Do not blame the lack of money for your mistakes, find the assertiveness of your newfound strength to believe that all you have to do is trust your own thinking and then ask for it. When you are hungry you eat and when you are tired you sleep, so why can't you think of money in the same way? If we ask for an advantage, we must be prepared to accept the responsibility for the completeness of that action. Remember that the form of a thought totally depends on the mental images we create through our own designated intensity! Your thoughts are the ultimate consummation of you!

Find your inner strength so that you can overcome your fears with no judgment. Listen to your thoughts, see if your ego that is your left brain is trying to control your right brain; it is the rebellious teenager within you looking for the easy way out of its own quandary through deceiving its own responsibilities.

Fear is an ongoing occurrence; it is something that you manifest and allow to grow and control you from within. Fear is childish thinking; it is just a hiccup within where you are pulled backwards; grow up and accept the challenge that you have a reserve supply of confidence that will be available to you every moment of your existence.

Question: I have this lack of trust in me to be worthy of money. I cannot even imagine what it's like to have lots of money. I want it, but I can't visualize having it.

Answer: If you can't imagine having it then you won't get it. Go back into your stillness, which is that state of silence within yourself, and work on creating a vision of your future. You must learn to become both judge and jury of yourself. When you think a thought to the universe you are talking to your own higher mind so look for the answer within; that God/Higher Self within, is on your side.

Question: I am waiting for the universe to give me the money to become self-employed; I haven't got enough capital to start the business with.

Answer: Fine, sit and wait Sir! But, if you would like to take just one step forward all by yourself, then the universe will work with you. It is like a rainbow connection to money. If you can become that rainbow then your business will become your light. When you are afraid of money and taking yourself back into the darkness of your fear, the universe cannot help you because it cannot see you in the dark; there is no light coming from you. You have to learn to earn yourself.

When you have decisions to make, remember that your first thought is always your best thought. Accept the first decision that you come to and then close the door on that question; do not stop to judge the decision. A decision is a divine energy that you have come to accept within yourself through your respect of self.

To become a winner is to serve our self, but to become a servant means that we have upheld ourself through our own consequences. To be of service to self, means that we are able to act on our own behalf and if we do that when we have the belief in self.

Question: It seems as though whenever I get money, I have to give it out again. Why is that?

Answer: If you work for your money why can't you keep just some for yourself? Write the word "future" on a glass jar/or a special account for the future and place your money in it. That money is not of this moment, it is for the future so it cannot be used. The word "future" is a word that is an expectation of what you can achieve. Keeping some money for yourself is going to change your life force towards your own expediency.

Start believing in yourself; that is the story of money!

At one stage of my journey when I was living and teaching in a Château in Europe, I had a staff of paid helpers. The Château had eight acres of parkland to keep in order, so the gardeners had a responsibility to uphold through my suggestions. The gardens were breathtaking; they were established, quiet, peaceful and serene. The trees were tall and majestic and were my boundary (they looked after and served me in their beauty). The Château was over 100 years old and was built strong and secure through the love of those who originally designed and lived there. It was constructed in perfect "Fung Schwa". The Château had four levels plus an attic. There were many rooms to be serviced; therefore, I required the staff to keep them in service for others.

There was one member of my staff who never had any money to call her own. When that lady staff member received her wages, through excitement she would go on a shopping rampage. One day that same staff member heard part of my seminar about money and requested that I help her to budget her money.

This is how I explained my teachings: If you want to buy something and you know what you want, then gift it to yourself. Make sure that you have twice the price of the gift in your purse, if not, then start saving. When you have achieved your savings result put half of the money into a jar/special account, then go out and enjoy spending the rest. That process begins to solidify in your aura and it builds itself up over time to work or walk itself back to you. The money in the jar/special account becomes the reserve bank; don't spend it. When we have achieved the results of our thinking the thought is then over.

The lady staff member wanted a new dishwasher. So, I explained to her to save double the cost of that dishwasher and when that was achieved, go out and buy it. Alternatively, you use half of the savings you have in your jar/special account as a deposit. Please take notice of how much money is in the jar/special account. After two years, the saving/spending routine eventually resulted in a lovely new car.

Start believing in yourself; that is the story of money! Listen to your thoughts and the words you speak!

During my studies, what I thought was truth I found was not. I was trained to watch a word and see how it continued to pull itself in and out of the truth. That word created its own reality according to the intention I gave it, or through the vibration of the word. When we sound a word, it echoes out into the consciousness. As that word echoes around it creates a vibration and that vibration moves and follows its own intention in a certain direction and takes the word along with it. That is a form of reality, but it was the myth that created the reality. Please realise, that reality is just in the moment and money follows the same theme.

Balance yourself and be still, and when you are ready to make your mark know that when you put that thought out into the universe it will be returned tenfold. If you ask for money in a balanced mind, money is what you will be given. Think of money as gold and become that gold in your mind. If your continual moment of gold is there with respect then your gold will last forever. Love your gold and it will love you.

A nugget of gold does not just come to the surface of the earth by itself; it is pushed or empowered from behind. It will sit there until the right energy equalizes it and if you are that lucky one to be there at the right time, then the nugget is yours. Gold is the same as your intelligence; you have to yearn to learn to earn it!

Money starts to flow automatically through you having put your mind or your intention to it. Remember that the unconscious/higher mind is there to react as a catalyst to your inner chatter, until you have completed the education of enlightenment and have finally understood yourself! From here on in, you become the catalyst for others. As you release your information to assist them, it is the natural law, that the universe assists you. It is amazing to note the changes that release in your life when you are in total acceptance of every thought you release! Don't restrict your truth, think of money releasing itself to you, through the freedom that you have upheld through reaching your own attainment.

In order to grow you must obtain and release all of the necessary facts through your own Individual Universal Law for your future growth. You are the Ritual, and the word "ritual" through the Sacred Alphabet means: Through Releasing my Intelligence, my Truth Understands and Ascends my Life. That means, everything that I think, I bring in and live in this moment. This is your instantaneous reality! It is returning your basic principles to you. Become your own ritual, where there is no place for the ego to reside in. "I am everything I think" is very easy to say. Remember your character is not a game of chance; it is the ultimate result of your continuous appraisal and effort. Ask for whatever you want and whatever you have earned will rightfully be returned to you. By you reading this chapter on money, you are investing in your quest of your own intelligence, where you will realize that you have no limits as to discovering your outer boundaries, which guides the way to your future.

Your Notes:

CHAPTER THIRTY TWO

Introduction To Metaphysical Numerology

Condensed excerpt from the book: "Decoding The Sacred Alphabet And Numerology", Chapter 26. Numerology, O.M. Kelly.

All numbers are powerful, when you fully understand the value of the thought that they must work with. The numbers of your birthday add up to a language of the responsibility you have the opportunity to uphold. The Divinity of Numbers, works through the intelligence of the Metaphysical language which is registered through the higher mind. It is through the acceptance of numbers that we are introduced up into the Sacred Geometry. It creates a structure, where we can conform and become all things through using the strength of our numbers, one digit at a time. Each number is created through a resonance that empowers itself, alerting the conscious, subconscious, and unconscious/higher minds – all of which multiplies through this additional intellect, and we learn to harmonize our thoughts with our self and with one another.

Allow me to initiate you into explaining the Shamanic Inheritance of numbers and their meanings.

1. I Am.

2. My Relationship; comes through acknowledging myself.

3. My Mind; is everything I am.

4. My Temple; my inner self; my education into discovering my darkness and my light.

5. My Freedom; I earn through the changes I have made to my self.

6. My Mastering; the gathering of one's self to master the understanding of all thought. Our ego loses its control over us when we accept the responsibility for every

thought that we think. Can you see how 666 became the mark of the beast? It is not negative; it is a powerful number which informs us of the responsibility we have to live up to in order to know our own mind.

7. My Communication; it is our intuition; it belongs to our teacher within. It produces our light, which we have labelled our Christ consciousness. This number is also in relationship to the knowledge of the angelic realms.

8. My Balance and Harmony; this is the sign of infinity; where everything is available and waiting for you.

9. My Death; to my old ways, through the education of my understanding and knowing all.

0. My Soul; my Alpha and Omega.

When the numbers become double digits, we relate to the above and bring them together.

10. I Am my Soul.

11. I Am as I Am.

12. I Am my Relationship.

And so on, throughout the numbers. Thus, we are affirming and collecting our intellect with each digit.

When the numbers vibrate into the twenties, it is through the connection to the number two (2), which represents the relationship we can attain through self. When we reach up to the thirties, we are opening up into the mind of self; we are embellishing ourselves to our mind. The forties are much higher, and they begin to collect up into the temple of self. This is where we never try to repeat our mistakes. Both brains (left, ego, conscious – right, emotions, subconscious) are realizing their intelligence, and this is where we are being tested through the consciousness to abstain from thinking in a negative way. We are beginning to enter up into the unconscious/higher recognition of our mind. The fifties are, through the changes of the old ways, where we are able to release to earn the freedom of self. The sixties are, through the gathering of self, where we begin to familiarize and master self. The seventies are the teachings of self, where we have the ability to unconsciously reflect our intellectual earnings out in order to teach others. The eighties are the harmonizing of self with the infinite, where we begin to prosper. The nineties are the belief of knowing self, where we have the ability to move into the next thought and/or attract ourselves up into the next world.

Each step of your intelligence that you awaken from its long, deep sleep advances outside your own reflection, where others are alerted to your energy, and it is also where you become aware of them, before they see you. They are waiting for you to move into their psyche, as they know that you can help them answer their questions. Once they learn to understand themselves, they then move into yours. The world is full of beauty and grace, isn't it? We are always in the right place at the right moment. When I was collaborating with all of this ultra mathematics during my training, my heart ached so much at the wonderment of how these Universal Laws are always permanently working on our behalf. This gave me so much more confidence, and it opened my heart up to where I could understand how to release myself into the arms of the creator of all things.

When we have three repetitions of the number one (i.e., 111), we are starting to collect the mind together. We begin here by looking at the number one (1), which is "I am", and, as there are three repetitions, we realize that this denotes as, "I am my mind". The "I am" is being reminded of your awakening, and now you must make an important decision to trust yourself more and move forward into the relationship of self – that is, you must not keep on thinking that your mind is in charge of you.

CHAPTER THIRTY THREE

The Quest Of Life

Everything the human mind creates through the power of just one thought is your unlimited access to the complete understanding, acceptance, and creation of your life.

To continue, this life quest or life program of yours keeps on creating itself through each of your thoughts building upon the other, and transformation continues until you have taken your last breath. That energy force field (life force) grows in strength and opens you up into your Higher – or heavenly – Self. That Higher Self follows you through every thought you think, always encouraging you to create and expand your thinking. We also call that Higher Self the unconscious/higher mind; its deliverance is always available, and it is permanently on standby. Its Higher Self is what we know as the Collective Consciousness. We cannot send it away; it is always there, silently watching and guiding us until we ask ourselves a question, and then it is up to us to receive and hear the message.

The Quest is your life unfolding itself through you looking at you! That is the cycle of life. Every human is doing this journey whether they are aware of it or not.

The quest for you to accept your next level of intellectual education means that you must move beyond your ego, where you will learn to harmonize your depleted emotions. As you climb intellectually higher to stimulate your emotions, your ego realizes that, all of a sudden, no one is in attendance to it! It has run out of its own energy, as you are no longer referring back to the past. Your newly found grace has brought you forward to where you have no wish to turn back! Therefore, you will become that much more powerful. Always remember this, though: On this Quest of Life, power does not mean control. Power can only be attained through strength as it is resurrected from within; that is, through your balancing both brains in the moment, not necessarily through your voicing authority over others. We can present to others only after we have received for ourselves.

Your mind is not your brain; your mind is the written word that is inscribed in every cell of your body (i.e., the Collective). Your mind and brain are two different elements that work as one, and yet have the strength to nourish and nurture one another, once the left and right hemispheres of our brain learn to accept and balance. When left and right are in balance, the mind and brain equate with one another through the sonic sound that produces the language of the unconscious/higher mind. You have the opportunity to reprogram your mind through understanding the unconscious recognition of Fung Shwa. You have now entered up into the royal-ness of self; you are collecting your own parliament.

The more respect we give to ourselves, the more our thoughts have the ability to strengthen. That is the Law of Attraction. Our illusion pulsates and creates the hidden strength of our own reflection. Through earning the stillness within the self, the vibration of trillions of your cells attracts attention to you. Stillness alerts the unconscious/higher mind. This is how we learn to accept the continuance to enter up into the next dimension of our reality.

In reference to the third dimension the three metaphysical dimensions of what we refer to as the "Mind of God" are called "EL-AN-EA" – representing the first Metaphysical God "EL" (Everlasting Life), which represents the home of our ego in relationship to our sexual encounters. These encounters are our basic structure of searching for a placement of our own responsibilities. This is the first doorway to where we connect to our lungs of consciousness, which is where we understand the breath of our inner worlds.

Our next evolution is into the Metaphysical God "AN" (Accepting and Nourishing), where we have understood our primordial earlier worlds through collecting our intelligence and accepting the possibilities of harvesting the seeds we have already sown (our thoughts and deeds). You have entered up into your education system, which is your inner university. Automatically, this subconscious awakening brings the information up to your heart, which opens you up into a belief that you can accomplish anything your mind desires. The combination of this energy then traverses up to connect us into the highest form of intelligence – our unconscious mind/ Higher Self – that is, to the Divinity of the Metaphysical God "EA", which, through the earlier language, was pronounced "He-ia" (Heavenly Energy of Intelligence Ascending). This is the last of the three prime Metaphysical Gods that we connect to, and it is the home of our heavenly kingdom, which is situated around the crown of the head. It is where we realize that God/Universe has a purpose for each and every one of us, and that we have the ability to reconnect back into the origin of our Soul. The fourth dimension opens up once we have accepted the other three, and through their support to look through our illusion, not at it.

When we step up into the fourth dimension, we are on another dimensional reality of intelligence, where we are learning to move into the acceptance of using the thinking of the right brain. We bring the old word of Feng Shui up into the higher vibration of Fung Shwa, where we vibrate through a different pulse, tone, and sound.

Stubbornness means the "rejection of one positive thought"; so the amount of stubbornness we create over what we are thinking determines the speed we "Fung and Shwa" the eternal energy through our mind. Stubbornness is created when we refuse to speak the thought in the moment, through our own premonition of losing control. Stop hanging on, and allow yourself to walk through your fear; this is where you can walk through your experiences to find out what you have yet to realize regarding your past. Once that is achieved, you can accept each thought in the moment. If only humanity understood how important this Quest of Life is; it shows us all to remember who we are.

There is one Universal Law that I would like you to always remember, and it is this: When you have accomplished something and earned it, it is then time to move on. You must keep the Law of Balance in your mind – do not hold it to you, as that will automatically put the brakes on tomorrow, and your ego will then want to take control of you again. "Not on!" says God/Collective Consciousness. This is how the Laws of Karma reconstruct the destruction that is felt by all.

As one cell ignites from one of your thoughts; it then echoes a beam of light throughout the whole body, through the emotion that you were feeling at that time, which helped you create that thought. If it comes through the left brain – which is the character of self that we admit to, in front of others – it releases on an outer level. If it comes through the right brain – which is when you speak to your core, or your Soul – it returns back into you. Through the stillness, it is an autonomic reaction from the teacher within. Therefore, you are always at the top of your class!

Consider this example: The pressure we put inside the pneumatic shock absorbers of a car determine how smoothly the car glides over bumpy roads. It is the pressure in the shock absorber that takes the bump, not the car itself. I learned that through driving on the Outback roads of Australia, some of which I would never want to journey over twice!

Through understanding the responsibility of your right brain, you have the emotional support to unravel the left. For Fung Shwa to react in the mind, it is important for us to understand that in order to know all, we must know our self! This journey does not balance itself until we mirror one brain to the other; the reflection between the two automatically creates harmony throughout the whole body.

Fung Shwa is where we bring every aspect of our energetic light (life force) into the oneness, through accepting the balance act, which you create in the moment. Being "in the light" means that you are forming a web – or net – of your own consciousness up into the Collective, which relays all around the planet. Each time you think a thought in your truth, that thought attracts attention; somebody out there waits for the support of that thought. This is how the feldic (from the German word "Feld", which means "field") grid forms around the planet; how it mathematically builds and creates the emotional balance, which is the telepathic vibration that creates the reasoning behind your thoughts.

As we think a thought, it attracts somebody just slightly

below us in vibration, and as that person thinks his/her own thought, it then attracts the next vibration down. The lower the frequencies become, the more its power is distributed out into the Collective. It is interesting to note how that vibration works. It is the Fung of the Shwa, and the Shwa of the Fung, that urge it forward. Just like the metronome works with music. The emotional vibration is in the moment; it weaves itself around the earth, and this enquiring energy is never-ending, always moving throughout the layers of the Collective in order to search for its home base.

Always remember, if you have not brought one of your thoughts into balance, someone else will claim it! Please endure with me; I know that my repetition of explaining things will strike a note of concordance that will automatically lift you up into the higher fields of energy, where it will work on your behalf!

Accept my words slowly, and allow them to digest; this will happen when you read the same thing over and over again, or when you hear the same word repeated. To enter up into the ethereal realms is like beginning your life all over again. You are innocently releasing your inner child. These words become a part of you, when you allow the nourishment of the unconscious/higher mind to return back through your emotional inheritance – your subconsciousness – and back into the conscious thought.

Your ego and emotions will learn to balance with each other. Take your time! I am showing you how the thousands of thoughts that you are capable of experiencing will allow you to accept yourself with clarity, and that clarity will embed itself deep within you. Those thoughts become personality references, your intellectual light that you can use throughout your own design. Paragraph by paragraph, I am reseating you through to understanding and receiving the benefits of all that you can become.

The prismatic formations of your thoughts form a complete web around the planet – not only in group energy, but more importantly, through self-realization. This is exactly what we mean when we pronounce the word reincarnation. When we die and reseat ourselves back into our own exposure, our original blueprint – or DNA – fractionalizes us back into the consciousness.

The dark thoughts that we often use as our excuses will overpower the light when we are not facing our inner truth of self; we then begin again to bring them both into a balance. The dark creates the matter, and the light is the antimatter. To create time, we cannot have time in matter; it is matter plus antimatter, and the equalization of both, that creates our progress through the movement of time.

With every thought you think, you are permanently reaching out and bringing your future to you; therefore accept that you are the Fung! The energy of your Shwa is collected and stored in your unconscious/higher mind, not in your conscious or subconscious minds. As we collect a thought to think, we create a vibration of energy that is collected up into the storehouse of the unconscious/higher mind, where the results are the Shwa!

Remember you are the most important person on the earth. Thank you for reading my story.

Your Notes:

Books By O.M. Kelly (Omni)

Decoding The Mind Of God
Author O.M. Kelly's seminal work, "Decoding the Mind of God", is a compilation of nine volumes of metaphysical information based on the research into the coded information of the Laws of the Universe, also known as the Collective Consciousness, and represents a groundbreaking contribution to our understanding of the metaphysical universe. Now, all nine volumes are being released as separate, revised books, each offering a unique perspective on the universe's workings. Omni's work has been widely acclaimed for its depth of insight, and her contributions to the field of metaphysics have been groundbreaking.
The nine separate volumes encompassing:

The Laws of the Universe
Thought
Dis-Ease
Death
Sexuality and Spirituality
The Dolphin's Breath
Sacred Alphabet and Numerology
Sacred Fung Shwa
Extra-Terrestrial Intelligence
*Updated version of each book, now being released separately.

Book I. Decoding The Laws Of The Universe
If you're looking to unlock the hidden potential within you and transform your life, "Decoding the Laws of the Universe" is the book for you. This powerful and insightful book is designed to help you understand the deeper, metaphysical aspects of life and tap into the transformative power of the universe utilising the secrets of our Individual Universal Law.

This book serves to introduce you into the secrets of our Individual Universal Law. This amazing knowledge and wisdom, is transformative on a personal level and creates the opportunity for you to interrelate with the Laws of the Universe. Throughout this book, you will dive deep into the inner workings of your mind and discover the hidden laws that govern your life. You will learn about the alchemy of the mind and how to harness its power to create positive change in your life and the world around you. Through the lens of Metaphysical philosophy, you will gain a new perspective on the world and your place in it. You will learn how the universe communicates with you through coded intelligence and how to unlock the hidden messages that are all around you.

This book is a journey for personal transformation and spiritual growth. Take a voyage of exploration of the expansive vistas of information discovering the codes of Metaphysics and the Quest of Life. You will learn the Metaphysical coded wisdom of the ancients for the necessary mind elements to transit into a higher mindset. Explore the secret relationship between the Earth and human beings, the higher mind, the Metaphysical journey, the importance of self, belief in self, the codes of mythology, a higher level of attainment, releasing the past, fears and evolving one's light on a Metaphysical level, what causes stress, work place promotion and why it does not happen, and many other topics. Included is a short overview of the conventional Twelve Laws of the Universe.

<u>Book II. Decoding Thought</u>
Welcome to a journey of self-discovery and exploration of the mysteries of the universe. "Decoding Thought" is a groundbreaking book that explores the power of the mind and the principles of metaphysical thought. Through a deep exploration of the mind and body connection, the author provides readers with insights to unlock the full potential of their thoughts. This book provides a guide to harnessing the power of the mind to create the life you desire. With explanations of metaphysical principles, the book makes these often complex concepts accessible to readers. "Decoding Thought" takes you on a journey through the vast landscape of the human mind. Explore the mysteries of thought power, and how it can shape our reality and transform our lives. The power of thought is not just a theoretical concept. It is a tangible force that can be harnessed to bring about significant changes in our lives.

This book can expand your consciousness and open your mind to new possibilities. By exploring the metaphysical principles that underlie our existence, you can gain a new perspective on life and the world around you. This book provides through a metaphysical interpretation explanations into the various aspects of thought power, including how it is linked to our DNA, and the roles played by the pituitary and pineal glands in our thought processes. O.M. Kelly also explains the metaphysical language in reference to the codes of the Egyptian Philosophies, the Bible, myths, cultures, and how they connect to the power of thought. The journey continues with a deep dive into the inner Secret School of Metaphysics, where we discover the Alchemy of the Brain and the pathway to our truth. Discover the unconscious/higher mind, and our Life Quest, which opens the doors to the Psychometric Consciousness. Through the lens of metaphysical interpretation, you will gain a new perspective on the impact of thought on our mental and emotional states that includes a look at Depression, Coping with Change and how to retrain our brain patterns to be positive and moving forward for our Financial Abundance and manifesting prosperity. The book ends with a brief overview of the brain/mind, and a short Q&A on thought power. This metaphysical book on the power of thought is a guide to discovering your true potential and creating the life you desire.

"Decoding Thought" is a must-read for anyone seeking to unlock the full potential of their mind and harness the power of the universe to create a life of fulfilment and this book serves as an invaluable resource.

Book III. Decoding Dis-Ease
Introducing "Decoding Dis-Ease" a Metaphysical Interpretation into understanding the intricate web of factors that contribute to our health and well-being. From the author of several groundbreaking works on the interaction of the mind and body, this book delves into a wide range of topics related to dis-ease. It is a fascinating and insightful book that offers a fresh perspective on health and healing. It is a must-read for anyone interested in the mind-body connection.

Readers will be inspired to embark on a quest of discovering the codes within themselves, recognizing that every cell in our body is pure Cosmic Consciousness. They will also gain a deeper understanding of specific health topics such as the thyroid, the kidneys, men's problems, and many other topics from a Metaphysical perspective. The book also examines how a disease is given to us in group energy and the complex interplay between our bodies and minds, and how every human has the consequences of all that we do and experience.

Book IV. Decoding Death

Looking for a thought-provoking exploration of death and the afterlife? Look no further than O.M. Kelly's book, "Decoding Death".

"Decoding Death takes us on a transformative Metaphysical journey through the mysteries of the Universe. O.M. Kelly—known as Omni—provides an expanded horizon of possibilities, awareness, and a transformative perspective. In this book, Omni delves into a wide range of topics related to dying and death, from the loss of a loved one to a viewing of the afterlife. Omni has a unique ability to view the Laws of the Universe using her extraordinary state of heightened awareness and multi-dimensional perception and through the lens of metaphysics offers a unique perspective on the nature of death and what it means for the human experience.

Omni shares personal experiences and stories, including the passing of her late husband, brother, and parents, and offers a metaphysical insight for those dealing with loss and grief. She explores the transformational process of death and the potential for spiritual growth and enlightenment. The book explains that the human experience of death is part of a larger Universal process that is ultimately guided by a higher intelligence referred to as God (Laws of the Universe/Collective Consciousness) or whatever name you prefer. Omni's exploration of death is both metaphysically comprehensive and thought-provoking, offering readers a deep and nuanced understanding of one of life's greatest mysteries. With chapters on the Three Doorways—Three Stages of Death, The Quantum Hologram—Why a partner dies for the other partner to progress in the "Journey of Life", The Passing to the Afterlife, and many other enlightening chapters, "Decoding Death" offers a unique viewpoint. By drawing on a range of religious, philosophical, and metaphysical perspectives, Omni offers a compelling vision of the human experience of death and its role in the larger Universal Law.

Book V. Decoding Sexuality And Spirituality

Welcome to "Decoding Sexuality and Spirituality" by O.M. Kelly. In this book, explore the fascinating relationship between our sexuality and spirituality, and how these two aspects of ourselves are intimately intertwined. Delve into the concept that sexuality is the doorway to our spirituality, and examine the powerful and transformative energy that is generated when we fully embrace our sexual selves. The book also explores the notion of the metaphysical orgasmic cloud, and how it can be used to deepen our connection to our spiritual selves. We will also examine the role of marriage in our sexual and spiritual lives.

For women, the book offers a unique perspective on the journey of embracing sexuality and spirituality, as well as insights into the different stages of life and how they impact our sexual and spiritual selves. Drawing on both ancient wisdom traditions and metaphysical mythology, the book examines the myth of Hercules and how it relates to our sexual intelligence. By decoding the symbolism of this myth, we can gain a deeper understanding of the ways in which our sexuality and spirituality intersect and influence each other. So if you are ready to embark on a journey of self-discovery and unlock the true potential of your sexual and spiritual selves, then "Decoding Sexuality and Spirituality" is the book for you.

Book VI. Decoding The Dolphin's Breath

"Decoding The Dolphin's Breath" by O.M. Kelly (Omni) is a captivating exploration of the relationship between humans and dolphins. The book begins with a poignant account of a real-life encounter between the author and a group of wild dolphins, setting the stage for a deep dive into the spiritual and metaphysical significance of dolphins. This captivating book takes readers on a journey into the heart of the dolphin-human relationship, exploring the ways in which these majestic creatures can help us attune to the power of free will, and telepathic communication.

Throughout the Laws of Shamanism the wonderful Dolphin in consciousness, represents the attainment we can reach through ourselves earning our freedom of will. This book explains the benefits of the dolphins breath—the why and how we use the breath that influences our divine mentality. Further, it's a story which reveals how the dolphins have taught us the process to be free of fear, and to tap into the Language of Babylon—to understand the language of Earth. One of the key themes of the book is the idea that dolphins are always breathing their total freedom of thought, and the author provides insights into how humans can learn from this remarkable trait. The book also invites readers to embark on a journey into understanding the telepathic communication of whales and dolphins. Inclusive in the book is a written meditation which assists you to connect to the external consciousness and release the fear that you have wrapped around yourself for protection.

Overall, this book offers a unique and fascinating perspective on the metaphysics of dolphins, and will appeal to anyone interested in spirituality, and the power of the mind.

Book VII. Decoding The Sacred Alphabet And Numerology
This book offers a myriad of explanations concerning the higher consciousness in relationship to names, places and numbers. "Decoding The Sacred Alphabet & Numerology" by O.M. Kelly (Omni) is a thought-provoking and enlightening read that offers a unique perspective on the metaphysical world of letters and numbers.

Omni's insights and teachings are sure to inspire readers to deepen their understanding of the ancient sacred codes to names of places, your name and the sacred alphabet. The author also delves into the practice of metaphysical numerology, which involves using numerical values to interpret personality traits, life paths, and other aspects of a person's life. Omni explains how metaphysical numerology can be used to gain insight into our spiritual path and to better understand our purpose in life. Your ability to decipher the Sacred Alphabet and Numerology codes commonly and constantly presented to you throughout your life, will open opportunities to expand your consciousness and awareness you never thought possible.

Embark on a journey through the myth of Babylon and

Shambhala and discover the sacred language that connects us all. Explore Luxor, the Delta Giza Saqqara and Faiyum, and Solomon's Temple, and uncover the mysteries of Akhenaton and Tomb KV-63. Find out how to unravel the threads of your DNA and unlock the ancient knowledge of the Old Aramaic Story of Aladdin and the Lamp. Explore Grecian stories through the Metaphysical language and travel along the Old Silk Road. Discover the Shamanic inheritance of numbers and their meanings, and learn how we rely on numbers to read the hidden language of the universe. Join O.M. Kelly on a journey of self-discovery and uncover the divine language within.

Book VIII. Decoding Sacred Fung Shwa
Introducing "Decoding Sacred Fung Shwa", the revolutionary guide to understanding and harnessing the energy within your home and yourself. In this book, author O.M. Kelly (Omni), has introduced a metaphysical sixth element that takes our understanding of energy to the next level. By incorporating "Your Life Force," we gain deeper insight into the connection between our homes and our emotional well-being. Discover the power of Fung Shwa and learn how to use it to create a balanced and harmonized environment that supports your mind, body, and Soul.

The book explains the meaning of Sacred Fung Shwa to the Shamanistic principles that underpin it. Delve into the metaphysical medicine wheel and explore the elements of life, before moving on to practical applications of Fung Shwa in the home.

Learn how to visualize your home as a collective energy and clear the clutter to enhance its flow. Discover your Astrological colours and how they can be used in Fung Shwa design, from the kitchen to the bedroom and beyond. Explore the compatibility of personal colours in relationships, and discover the power of paintings, pictures, and mirrors to enhance your home's energy.

But Fung Shwa isn't just about the home—we also explore its applications in the office environment and in small retail businesses. Learn how to apply Fung Shwa principles to a clothing store, shoe store, or café, even discover the role of Fung Shwa in money, and to Metaphysical Numerology.

Throughout it all, we focus on the quest of life and how Fung Shwa can help you achieve your goals and live your best life. So what are you waiting for? Dive into the world of Fung Shwa and transform your home, your business, and your life today!

Book IX. Decoding Extra-Terrestrial Intelligence

Are you ready to embark on a journey of self-discovery? Look no further than O.M. Kelly's groundbreaking book, Book IX "Decoding Extra-Terrestrial Intelligence". Through metaphysical interpretation, O.M. Kelly (Omni) has unlocked the secrets of the universe and revealed that the key to our next step in human evolution lies within ourselves. This book will show you how to tap into the indelible imprint of holographic importance that is seeded within every human, and unleash the Extra-Terrestrial Intelligence that resides within you. Omni shares her own personal journey of encountering Beings of Light and how it has transformed her understanding of the universe and humanity's place within it.

Omni presents the concept that we all have Extra-Terrestrial Intelligence, and have the ability to tap into the vast knowledge and secrets of the universe. The ancient civilizations left behind clues and teachings about this metaphysical existence and it is up to us to continue to uncover and advance the way we think.

Through this journey of life, we can unlock the secrets of our own consciousness and tap into the full potential of our existence. This is a fascinating exploration of the mysteries of the universe and the potential for our own personal evolution.

Readers who are interested in self-transformation through universal truths, Metaphysical exploration for personal growth and a journey of self-discovery would be interested in reading this insightful book on contact with Beings of Light and Extra-terrestrial Intelligence, exploring ancient civilizations and the knowledge they possessed about the universe and the human mind.

Power Thought For The Day Oracle Book

"Power Thought For The Day Oracle Book" provides insights to assist you on your life path. Through the "Totem" energy of all, the ancient species that have evolved before us, represent an emotional inheritance that we can rely on to sustain the moment. Each species that has evolved on this planet is recorded into our cellular memory. This book with 22 Major Arcana Shamanic Power Animal Totems provides a contemporary metaphysical interpretation symbolic of our evolution. By selecting a page of the book the Shamanic animal will provide an insight in how you are thinking at this moment in time. Through the contemporary Laws of Shamanism (with a metaphysical interpretation), O.M. Kelly (Omni) has produced a book that will assist the "Path of the Initiate" in emotional intelligence when our mind is in the field of doubt. When we become aware of how we are thinking it is a catalyst for transformation. This compact little book is a handy 4 x 7 inches or 10.2 x 17.8 cm to fit into your pocket or handbag.

How to use the book:
Our higher mind has no time; it steps into and works on behalf of the thought of the moment. This book encompasses 22 Major Totem Power representations, symbolic of our evolution. Close your eyes and inhale and exhale a deep breath and relax and allow yourself no thought as you select the right page of the Shamanic animal presented in this book. The right page will always appear for you at the right moment and you will discover how the power animals are working with you for insight into their wisdom. Different power animals come into our lives at various phases offering messages to guide us on our path.

Decoding The Shaman Within

In "Decoding the Shaman Within" international author O.M. Kelly (Omni) shares her Shamanic metaphysical journey. It would be termed a contemporary Shamanic initiation journey; a powerful spiritual enlightenment and transformational voyage of discovering the codes of Metaphysics and the Quest of Life. Through the sacred passage of time Omni discovered the secret codes of the Collective Consciousness (Laws of the Universe) to trek a higher level of consciousness. Throughout

Omni's training to receive the breath of Shamanism, many Elders from other cultures came to Australia and initiated her into their own tribal laws. Most of these Elders were men who arrived on Omni's doorstep uninvited but had received the call from the Universe to pass on their knowledge. Those magnificent people who had also earned their Shamanic experiences, only stayed long enough to give Omni their gift of consciousness and to initiate her into a new Shamanic name, which their tribe had bestowed, and then they disappeared out of Omni's life as quickly as they had come into it.

The Shamanic path in a Metaphysical perspective is the oldest pathway of the tribal law through the evolution of humanity. The Shaman is trained in the ancient language that is instilled in every genetic code that humanity carries within their DNA; you either have the opportunity to open it up and use it, or you just don't bother and choose to ignore it! It is as simple as that!

Decoding The Revelation Of Saint John The Divine: Understand The Role You Inherit
The amazing breakthrough book "Decoding the Revelation of Saint John the Divine: Understand the role you inherit", is for anyone with an open, inquiring mind, seeking answers to the surreal descriptions of Earth's final days. Through years of research O.M. Kelly interprets the cryptology behind the codes of mythology and various religions and has Metaphysically interpreted how the Holy Bible had been written through the original codex of Egyptology. The biblical stories were collected and condensed through the educated minds of that time.

Decoding The Ten Plagues Of Egypt
"Decoding the Ten Plagues of Egypt" presents a fresh insight into understanding the hidden structure of the language of how the Bible was written. The reader is introduced to the step by step Metaphysical decoding of the mystifying language, regarding the plagues from the Book of Exodus, Chapters: 7-12 in the Bible.

For the first time in contemporary history the essence of the Book of Exodus and its previously unsolved intriguing language will be revealed to provide deeper knowledge and clearer perception to unlock the significance the Book of Exodus is explaining to us.

Decoding Dreams
In "Decoding Dreams" international author O.M. Kelly (Omni), introduces a metaphysical interpretation of the dreams we dream. At times, we may believe that dreams allow us to peer into another world. O.M. Kelly provides the codes for us to understand that other world of dreams—or, through the Shamanic Principles, our "Vision Worlds". Dreams are created through your unconscious/higher mind communicating back to you; dreams are reminding you of the lessons that you need to understand regarding yourself. You cannot hear them if your mind is filled with incessant chatter. The ego refuses to conform when it is in control of the moment. Dreams can range from a pleasant dream, which could be a recommendation to add to what you are doing, to a nightmare, which is a wake-up call from your higher self regarding what you are doing to yourself. As you read this book, keep in mind that learning to metaphysically interpret your dreams is a step-by-step process. Areas covered in the book are: Dream Representations (Animal Kingdom and the Human Kingdom), Questions and Answers about Dreams, and Dream Interpretations.
*Reprint coming in the near future.

www.ingramcontent.com/pod-product-compliance
Lightning Source LLC
Chambersburg PA
CBHW062037290426
44109CB00026B/2653